mentor „sehr gut"

Englisch: sehr gut

5. Klasse

Gymnasium und Gesamtschule

Susan Bollinger
Angela Drude-Moss
Carola Jeschke

Mit Download für phase-6

Einfach ins Langzeitgedächtnis

In Zusammenarbeit mit Langenscheidt

mentor
Eine Klasse besser.

Die Autorinnen

Susan Bollinger, M.A., ist Diplomübersetzerin und unterrichtet ihre Muttersprache Englisch seit vielen Jahren an der Universität München; sie hat außerdem umfangreiche Unterrichtserfahrung an deutschen Schulen und als Nachhilfelehrerin und ist Autorin einiger Lernhilfen.

Angela Drude-Moss unterrichtet ihre Muttersprache Englisch seit vielen Jahren an der Universität München und hat außerdem mehrjährige Erfahrung in der Lehrerausbildung und im Nachhilfeunterricht.

Carola Jeschke ist Gymnasiallehrerin für Englisch und Deutsch und seit vielen Jahren mit der Erarbeitung von Unterrichtsmaterialien in beiden Fächern befasst.

Projektbetreuung: bookwise medienproduktion, München
Redaktion: Carolin Wolf, Regensburg
Layout: Cordula Schaaf, München
Umschlaggestaltung: Design im Kontor – Iris Steiner, München
Zeichnungen: Sabine Völkers, Berlin
Lerneinheiten für den Download: Carola Jeschke

www.mentor.de
www.mentor.de/sehr-gut

Umwelthinweis: Gedruckt auf chlorfrei gebleichtem Papier.

Satz: Ute Konstanzer, München
Repro: Lana Repro, Lana
Gesamtherstellung: Druckerei A. Plenk, Berchtesgaden
Printed in Germany

ISBN 978-3-580-65225-8

1. 2. 3. 4. 5. 13 12 11 10 09

Inhalt

1 Nomen und Pronomen

1.1 Nouns/Nomen 6
1.2 Articles/Artikel 8
1.3 Genitive/Genitiv 10
1.4 Pronouns and Determiners/Pronomen und Begleiter 11
Abschlusstest 16

2 Zeiten

2.1 The Simple Present/Die einfache Gegenwart 20
2.2 The Present Progressive/Die Verlaufsform der Gegenwart 24
2.3 The Simple Past/Die einfache Vergangenheit 26
Abschlusstest 29

3 Satzformen

3.1 The Statement/Der Aussagesatz 32
3.2 Questions/Fragen 36
3.3 Imperatives/Befehlsform 40
3.4 Subordinate Clauses/Nebensätze 41
Abschlusstest 42

4 Zahlen, Uhrzeit, Datum

4.1 Numbers/Zahlen 46
4.2 Time/Uhrzeit 50
4.3 Dates/Datumsangaben 53
Abschlusstest 55

5 Angaben zu Ort, Zeit, Häufigkeit

5.1 Adverbial Phrases of Place/Ortsangaben 58
5.2 Adverbial Phrases of Time/Zeitangaben 59
5.3 Adverbial Phrases of Frequency/Häufigkeitsangaben 62
Abschlusstest 63

6 Präpositionen

6.1 Prepositions of Time/Präpositionen der Zeit 66
6.2 Prepositions of Place/Präpositionen des Ortes 68
6.3 Prepositions of Direction/Präpositionen der Richtung 70
Abschlusstest 73

7 Leseverstehen

7.1 Reading and Understanding/Lesen und Verstehen 76
Abschlusstest 79

8 Wortschatz und Situationen

8.1 Den Wortschatz sichern und erweitern 82
8.2 Situationen meistern 90
Abschlusstest 93

Lösungen

1 Nomen und Pronomen 96
2 Zeiten 101
3 Satzformen 105
4 Zahlen, Uhrzeit, Datum 109
5 Angaben zu Ort, Zeit, Häufigkeit 112
6 Präpositionen 114
7 Leseverstehen 118
8 Wortschatz und Situationen 120

Wichtige unregelmäßige Verben 125
Stichwortfinder 127

★ Dieses Sternchen markiert Übungen und Regeln, die etwas anspruchsvoller sind oder nicht überall verlangt werden. Wenn du ganz sicher bist, dass du sie nicht brauchst, kannst du sie überspringen. Ansonsten gilt: Stell dich der Herausforderung!

1

Nomen und Pronomen

Mr and Mrs Johnson have three children, Katie, who is thirteen years old, and the twins, Mark and Mandy, who are just ten.

The Johnsons live in a nice house in a quiet road in Canterbury, a town in the county of Kent in the south-east of England with a famous cathedral. Mr Johnson works in a bank in the centre of Canterbury; Mrs Johnson works in the office of the local church.

1.1 *Nouns*/Nomen

Alles klar?! ***Nouns (Singular/Plural)*/Nomen (Singular/Plural)**

Fülle die Lücken aus und überprüfe deine Ergänzungen im Lösungsteil.

*Mark and Mandy are **twins**.*

Wenn man ein Nomen in den Plural (Mehrzahl) setzt, hängt man normalerweise ein ***-s*** an.

- Nach den harten, stimmlosen Konsonanten, z. B. *p, t, k,* spricht man das -*s* stimmlos aus.
- Nach weichen, stimmhaften Konsonanten, z. B. *b, d, d, l,* und Vokalen, spricht man das -*s* stimmhaft aus.

stimmlos		**stimmhaft**	
cat	....	*girl*	....
lamp	....	*boy*	....

*The **buses** from that stop go to the town centre.*

Wenn ein Wort auf einen **Zischlaut** ([s],[z],[tʃ], [dʒ]) endet, hängt man ***-(e)s*** an (ein -*s* allein könnte man gar nicht aussprechen). Das angehängte -*(e)s* spricht man [ɪz] aus.

bus	....	*watch*	....
house	....	*dress*	....

*Katie's **hobbies** are riding and reading.*

Wenn ein Nomen auf einen **Konsonanten + *-y*** endet, wird das *y* zu einem *ie*, die Endung lautet *-ies*.

baby	....	*hobby*	....

*The **potatoes** taste good.*
*They catch the **thieves**.*

Besondere Schreibweisen:

- Nomen auf *-o* fügen oft *-es* an: *tomato – tomatoes*.
- Nomen auf *-f* bilden den Plural oft mit *-ves: leaf – leaves*

Wie so oft, gibt es bei der Pluralbildung ein paar Ausnahmen, die man lernen muss:
man – men, women – women, child – children, tooth – teeth, foot – feet

Übung 1 **Ergänze die Lücken.**

Singular (Einzahl)	Plural
family	
	scarves
class	
sandwich	

	bridges
church	
	potatoes
knife	
	babies

Lösungen Seite 96

Alles klar?! ***Uncountable Nouns*/nichtzählbare Nomen**

*Mark likes **milk** very much.*

Es gibt Nomen, die man nicht in den Plural setzen kann, weil man die Dinge, die sie bezeichnen, nicht zählen kann.

*Mark has **two glasses of milk** every morning.*

Es gibt einen Trick, wie man unzählbare Nomen zählbar machen kann: Man ergänzt ein zählbares Nomen.

food	*a **bag** of food*	*water*	*a **glass** of water*
tea	*a **cup** of tea*	*work*	*a **piece** of work*

Alles klar?! ***Pair words*/Paarwörter**

*Katie's new **jeans** look really great.*

Paarwörter bezeichnen Dinge, die aus zwei gleichen Teilen bestehen (die Jeans sozusagen aus zwei Hosenbeinen). Sie werden deshalb nur im Plural verwendet, d. h., auch das Verb wird in den Plural gesetzt.

*Katie has got **five pairs of jeans.***

Wenn man Paarwörter zählbar machen will, so verbindet man sie mit ***pair of***.

Übung 2 **Kannst du die Wörter den Zeichnungen zuordnen? Setze die richtige Nummer zum Bild.**

1. You wear socks to keep your feet warm.
2. You wear gloves to keep your hands warm
3. Scissors are useful for cutting paper.
4. Women often wear elegant shoes.
5. In summer children wear shorts.
6. Glasses help you to see better.
7. Trousers are like shorts but longer.
8. You wear pyjamas to go to bed.

Übung 3 ★ **Übersetze die unterstrichenen Wörter ins Englische.**

1. Die Brille ist schmutzig. ....
2. Die Schere ist scharf. ....
3. Die Hose ist lang. ....
4. Der Schlafanzug ist rot. ....

Lösungen Seite 96

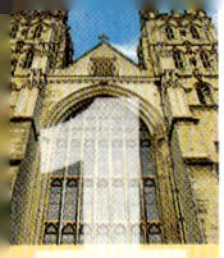

1.2 *Articles*/Artikel

Alles klar?! ***The Definite Article*/Der bestimmte Artikel**

***The** girl and **the** boy over there are Mandy and Mark.* ***The** two sisters like to wear jeans.*	Im Englischen braucht man nicht zu beachten, welches Geschlecht ein Nomen hat – es gibt nur einen Artikel, im Singular wie im Plural. Aussprache: [ðə] vor Konsonaten: *the boy, the girl* [ðɪ] vor Vokalen (a, e, i, o, u): *the uncle, the aunt*
*Mark plays **the recorder**.*	Manchmal braucht man im Englischen einen Artikel, wenn man im Deutschen keinen braucht. Übersetze den Satz in der linken Spalte: ....
*After **breakfast** the children leave the house for **school**.* *They go to **school** by bike.* *The Johnsons live in **Charlton Road**.* *The twins' birthday is in **May**.*	Umgekehrt braucht man manchmal im Englischen keinen Artikel, wenn man im Deutschen einen braucht. Suche Beispiele in den Sätzen links, bei denen im Englischen, anders als im Deutschen, kein Artikel steht: Mahlzeiten, z. B. .... Bezeichnungen von Gebäuden, wenn sie deren Funktion beschreiben, z. B. .... Straßennamen, z. B. .... Monate, z. B. ....

Übung 1 **Marks Freund Ben schreibt ihm eine Mail aus dem Urlaub. Füge den bestimmten Artikel in die Lücken ein, wo er gebraucht wird.**

Hi Mark,

Greetings from Wales! .... weather is not very good, but .... hotel is fine. It is not far from .... sea and has .... internet access. Every morning we have .... breakfast before 8 o'clock and then we go by .... bus to visit places in .... area. .... people here are very friendly, but .... language is difficult to understand. We often have to go into one of .... shops to ask for help. In .... evenings, after .... supper, we watch .... television or play .... cards. Hope, you are enjoying your holiday.

Love, Ben

Lösungen Seite 97

Alles klar?! ***The Indefinite Article*/Der unbestimmte Artikel**

In the Johnsons' garden there is ***a*** *plum tree and* ***an*** *apple tree.*
He is ***a*** *teacher.*

Wie beim bestimmten Artikel braucht man bei der Verwendung des unbestimmten Artikels nicht auf das Geschlecht der Nomen zu achten. Lediglich Aussprache und Schreibung werden wieder von den ersten Buchstaben der Nomen bestimmt.

a [ə] vor Konsonaten: *a plum, a boy, a girl*

an [ən] vor Vokalen *(a, e, i, o, u): an apple*

Übung 2 **Setze die richtige Form des unbestimmten Artikels ein.**

a) .... umbrella
b) .... banana
c) .... good book
d) .... young dog
e) .... interesting story
f) .... aeroplane
g) .... old house
h) .... bridge
i) .... orange
j) .... twin
k) .... animal
l) .... hobby

Canterbury

1.3 *Genitive*/Genitiv

Alles klar?! ***s*-Genitive and *of*-Genitive**

Katie's room *is on the first floor of the house.*	Wenn der Besitzer einer Sache eine Person oder ein Tier ist, verwendet man den ***s*-Genitiv**, d. h., man hängt einen **Apostroph** und ein ***s*** an das Nomen.
The twins' room *is next to Katie's room.*	Bei Nomen mit regelmäßigem Plural wird nur ein **Apostroph** angehängt – das zusätzliche ***s*** wäre ja überflüssig.
The children's *room is very big.*	Das gilt nicht für Nomen mit unregelmäßigem Plural: Hier braucht man, wie im Singular, Apostroph + *s*.
Mark and Mandy's *room has got a big window.*	Wenn eine Sache zwei Personen gehört, hängt man das *'s* nur bei der zweiten Person an.
The ***windows of the house*** *are very small.*	Wenn man ausdrücken will, dass eine Sache zu einer anderen Sache gehört, verwendet man den ***of*-Genitiv**.

Übung 1 **Finde den richtigen Weg durch den Irrgarten zu den Objekten, damit du schreiben kannst, wem was gehört.**

1. Ben's computer
2. ....
3. ....
4. ....
5. ....
6. ....
7. ....
8. ....

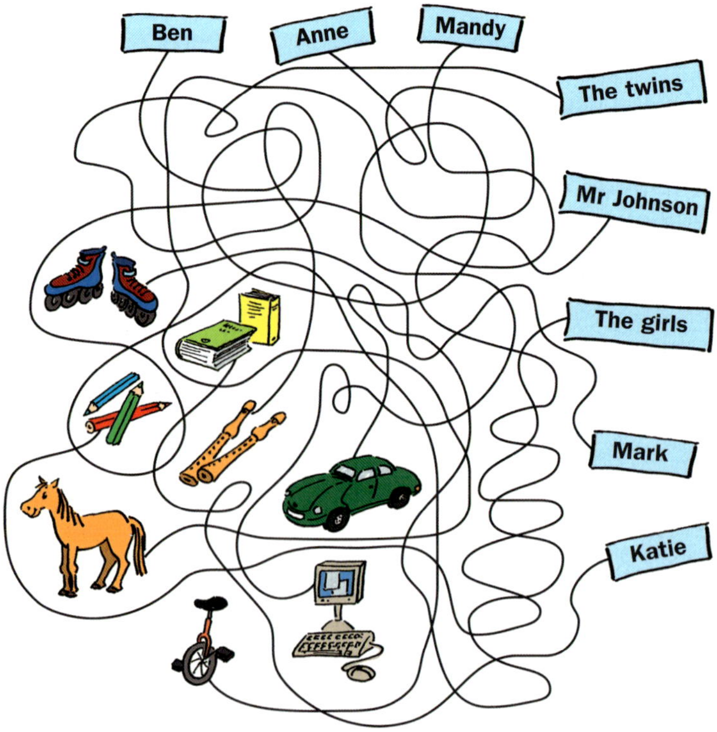

Lösungen Seite 97

1.4 *Pronouns and Determiners*/Pronomen und Begleiter

Alles klar?! ***Personal Pronouns (Subject Case)*/Personalpronomen (Subjektform)**

The Johnsons live in a nice house. → ***They** live in a nice house.*

Die **Subjektform** des Personalpronomens wird verwendet, wenn es das Subjekt (= Satzgegenstand) des Satzes ist. Man fragt nach ihnen mit *Wer?*.

Formen:

	Singular	**Plural**
1. Person	*I (like)*	*we (like)*
2. Person	*you (like)*	*you (like)*
3. Person	*he/she/it (likes)*	*they (like)*

Beachte: *I* wird immer großgeschrieben, ein kleines i würde im Text ja verschwinden.

The bus leaves at eight o'clock. → ***It** leaves at eight.*

Dinge sind im Englischen fast immer sächlich. Deshalb muss *it* verwendet werden.

Maggie is the Johnson's cat. → ***She** is very cuddly.*

Tiere können sächlich sein. Wenn man sie gut kennt, kann man auch *he* oder *she* verwenden.

Übung 1 **Setze die richtigen Pronomen ein.**

1. Mr Johnson works in a bank. .... works in a bank.
2. Mark and Mandy love Maggie, the cat. .... love Maggie.
3. Mrs Johnson works in an office. .... works in an office.
4. Katie is learning French. .... is learning French.
5. The cat catches mice. .... catches mice.
6. Mark and Mandy are twins. .... are twins.
7. Mother and I like cooking. .... like cooking.
8. The train for London leaves at twelve o'clock. .... leaves at 12 o'clock.
9. Mark asks Ben to send him an email. "Will .... send me an email, please?"
10. Katie asks the twins to feed Maggie. "Will .... feed Maggie, please?"

Lösungen Seite 98

Alles klar?! ***Personal Pronouns (Object Case)*/Personalpronomen (Objektform)**

Mark likes playing with Mandy. → He likes playing with ***her.***

Die Objektform des Personalpronomens wird verwendet, wenn es im Satz das Objekt ist. Man fragt danach mit *Wem?* oder *Wen?*.
Ergänze die deutschen Formen:

	Singular	Deutsch	Plural	Deutsch
1. Person	*me*	*mir/mich*	*us*	
2. Person	*you*		*you*	
3. Person	*him* *her* *it*		*them*	

Übung 2 **Ersetze die unterstrichenen Satzteile durch Personalpronomen.**

1. Please, give the book to Mandy. ....
2. Katie often plays with the twins. ....
3. These flowers are for Mrs Johnson. ....
4. Can you ring Mr Johnson at work, please? ....
5. The doctor is coming to see our family. ....
6. The teacher tells Mark and Mandy to do their homework. ....
7. Please, give Katie the magazine. ....
8. Ben writes Mark an email. ....

Eigentlich einfacher ...
Dass **Sachen sächlich** sind, ist ja eigentlich logisch, oder? Weil das im Deutschen nicht immer so ist, machen wir hier am Anfang manchmal Fehler, wenn wir Englisch lernen.
Der Bus ist im Deutschen männlich, wir sprechen von **er**.
Im Englischen ist ***the bus*** sächlich, also ***it***.

Lösungen Seite 98

Alles klar?! ***Possessive Determiners*/Possessivbegleiter**

Maggie is Mark and Mandy's cat.
→ It is ***their*** *cat.*

Possessivbegleiter zeigen Besitzverhältnisse an und stehen direkt vor dem Nomen.

Formen:

	Singular	Plural
1. Person	*my (cat)*	*our (cat)*
2. Person	*your (cat)*	*your (cat)*
3. Person	*his/her (cat)*	*their (cat)*

Mark hurt ***his*** *arm.*
Take off ***your*** *shoes.*

Bei Körperteilen und Kleidungsstücken müssen im Englischen Possessivpronomen verwendet werden.

Übung 3 **Setze die richtigen Personalpronomen (in der Objekt- und Subjektform) und die Possessivbegleiter ein.**

Katie schreibt ihrer neuen deutschen Brieffreundin Julia eine E-Mail und berichtet darin über ihre Familie.

Hi Julia,

.... name is Katie and .... am .... new penfriend from England. .... am thirteen years old. .... father is called Phil. .... is 45 years old. .... mother's name is Betty, ... is 40 years old. .... both go out to work. .... have a brother and a sister, ... names are Mark and Mandy and .... are twins. .... are only ten years old. We live in a quiet road in a big house. .... has a large garden with nice trees. .... also have a cat, ... is called Maggie. .... is black and white and loves to play in the garden. The twins say, Maggie is .... cat, I say, it is .... cat. I hope, ... can come for a visit soon, then .... will meet .... family.

Cheers,
Katie

Lösungen Seite 99

Alles klar?! ***Possessive Pronouns/*Possessivpronomen**

*The green t-shirt is **hers** and the yellow t-shirt is **his**.*

Possessivpronomen ersetzen das Nomen. Auch sie zeigen an, wem etwas gehört.

	Singular	**Plural**
1. Person	*mine*	*ours*
2. Person	*yours*	*yours*
3. Person	*his/hers*	*theirs*

Übung 4 **Ergänze die Sätze mit den richtigen Possessivpronomen.**

1. This is the Johnson's house. This house is ....
2. The twins are looking for their shoes, they ask: "Are these shoes ....?"
3. This book is not Katie's book, it belongs to me, it is ....
4. This basket is for Maggie. The basket is ....
5. Here is a new dress for you. The dress is ....
6. Mandy and Mark have bikes, the red one is .... and the blue one is ....

Lösungen Seite 99

Alles klar?! ***Demonstrative Pronouns/*****Demonstrativpronomen**

Mit Demonstrativpronomen oder hinweisenden Fürwörtern weist man, wie der Name sagt, auf etwas hin.

Wenn man auf Dinge hinweist, die nah sind, verwendet man:
Singular: *this* **Plural:** *these*

This *(here) is Katie's room.*
These *(here) are Katie's books.*

Wenn man auf Dinge hinweist, die weiter entfernt sind, verwendet man:
Singular: *that* **Plural:** *those*

That *(over there) is Mark and Mandy's room.*
Those *(over there) are their books.*

Übung 5 **Setze die fehlenden Demonstrativpronomen ein.**

	Singular	**Plural**
1.	this bike	.... bikes
2.	.... tree	those trees
3.	that girl	.... girls
4.	.... boy	these boys
5.	that house	.... houses
6.	.... cat	these cats
7.	that garden	.... gardens
8.	.... basket	these baskets
9.	that shoe	.... shoes

Lösungen Seite 99

Abschlusstest (25 Minuten)

STOPP! Zuerst die Lernkärtchen durcharbeiten!

Aufgabe 1 **Übersetze die unterstrichenen Wörter ins Englische.**

a) Katie fragte sie (die Zwillinge), ob sie Hausaufgaben aufhatten. ....

b) Mark und Mandy feiern ihren Geburtstag. ....

c) Die Katze spielt mit ihrem Ball. ....

d) „Katie, ist das dein Pferd?" ....

Punkte: ☐ von 4

Aufgabe 2 **Übersetze die unterstrichenen Personalpronomen.**

a) Das ist unser Garten. ....

b) Gibst du mir bitte den Ball. ....

c) Ich suche die Zwillinge. Hast du sie gesehen? ....

d) Mark: "Mandy, kannst du mich sehen? Ich sitze im Baum." ....

e) Wir sind die Johnson-Zwillinge. Zeigst du uns bitte unsere Plätze? ....

f) Wo ist Katie? Sie ist im Garten. ....

Punkte: ☐ von 6

Lösungen Seite 99

Aufgabe 3 **Ergänze die Lücken mit den richtigen Pronomen.**

a) Look, Mandy and Mark! .... are the Johnson twins. It is .... birthday and I have a present for ....

b) Mrs Johnson: "Katie, is this .... French book?" Katie: "Yes, Mum, can .... give it to me, please."

c) Mr Johnson is looking for .... briefcase, but .... can't find it.

d) "Who is .... girl over there? I don't know ....!"

e) "Are .... children over there Mark and Mandy?" "Yes, ... are playing in the garden with .... cat, Maggie."

f) The twins are angry with Katie, who says Maggie is .... cat. "She is not ...., she is ....," they shout.

Punkte: ☐ von 15

Aufgabe 4 **Setze, wenn notwendig, den bestimmten oder unbestimmten Artikel ein.**

Mark meets his friend Ben at the bus stop.

Ben: Hi Mark, are you going to .... school by .... bus today?

Mark: Yes, I normally go by .... bike, but my bike is broken. I hope to get .... new mountain bike for my birthday, but .... mountain bikes are expensive.

Ben: I have .... judo class after ....school today, why don't you come?

Mark: Thanks for .... invitation, but I can't come. My mother is at .... work today and I have to feed .... cat.

Ben: Can't Mandy do that? She is not at .... school today, is she at .... home?

Mark: No, she's in .... town. She's .... girl guide and has .... meeting at .... church in .... Market Street.

Ben: What a pity! I'm sure, we will have .... fun and after .... training we all go for .... hamburger.

Mark: Well, if my mother comes back from .... work early, maybe I can join you.

Ben: That's .... good idea. See you!

Punkte: ☐ von 22

Lösungen Seite 100

Aufgabe 5 **Übersetze die Sätze ins Englische.**

1. Das Haus der Johnsons ist in der Charlton Road.

....

2. Das Zimmer der Zwillinge hat ein großes Fenster.

....

3. Die Fahrräder der Kinder sind grün und rot.

....

4. Katies Zimmer ist sehr klein.

....

5. Die Klassenzimmer der Schule sind groß.

....

Punkte: ☐ von 10

Aufgabe 6 **Bilde Sätze mit dem Inhalt der Kästchen.**

Mandy has ....

....

....

....

2 x milk | 1 x scissors | 3 x pyjamas | 3 x jeans

Mark says ....

....

....

....

My shorts | The glass | The glasses | My trousers

are/is

empty | red | long | dirty

Punkte: ☐ von 8

Punkte: ☐ von 65

56–65: Bravo! Du weißt über die Nomen und Pronomen schon gut Bescheid.
40–55: Teilweise bist du sicher, teilweise noch nicht. Bearbeite bitte noch einmal die Übungen, in denen du beim ersten Mal viele Fehler hattest.
0–39: Leider ist dir noch zu vieles unklar. Arbeite das Kapitel bitte noch mal durch.

Lösungen Seite 100

2 Zeiten

The Johnson children attend different schools. Katie is in her second year at secondary school where she started learning French last year and has just started learning German. The twins are still at junior school in their last year. They are looking forward very much to going to secondary school, the same one as Katie attends, when the new school year starts in September.

2.1 *The Simple Present*/Die einfache Gegenwart

Alles klar?! **Bildung des *Simple Present***

Ergänze die Lücken.

*I **like** volleyball.*

Bei *I/you/we/they* verwendet man das Verb in der Grundform.
I like, you like, we like, they like

*My brother **likes** football.*

Bei der 3. Person Singular *(he/she/it)* hängt man ein .... an.
he likes, she likes, it likes

He/she/it – „s“ muss mit!

catch ↓ *He catch**es** the ball.*

*hurr**y*** ↓ *She hurr**ies** home.*

Beim Schreiben beachtet man besonders:

- Verben, die mit einem Zischlaut [s],[z],[tʃ], [dʒ] enden: Man hängt .... an.
- Verben, die auf Mitlaut (Konsonant) + *y* enden: Das *y* wird zu ...... , und man hängt .... an.

Weitere Verben mit unregelmäßiger Schreibung:
he goes, she does.

Übung 1 **Setze das jeweilige Verb in die richtige Form.**

I		(to work)
He		(to hurry)
We		(to sing)
She		(to wash)
They		(to eat)
You		(to like)
He		(to go)
I		(to see)
It		(to start)
She		(to fetch)

Lösungen Seite 101

Alles klar?! **Bildung von *to be***

	Langform		Kurzform	
	Singular	**Plural**	**Singular**	**Plural**
*I **am** (I'm) English.*	*I*	*we*	*I*	*we* ....
*He **is** (He's) in school today.*	*you*	*you*	*you*	*you* ....
*We/You/They **are** (We're/You're/They're) German.*	*he*	*they*	*he*	*they* ....
	she		*she*	
	it		*it*	

Übung 2 **Setze *to be* in die richtige Form.**

Mandy is talking to her brother Mark.

Mandy: We must hurry, we .... late for school. Where .... your school bag?

Mark: It .... in my room.

Mandy: Where .... your shoes?

Mark: They .... in the kitchen.

Mandy: Why .... you so untidy?

Mark: Because I .... always short of time.

Mandy: Well, that .... true for both of us now!

Übung 3 ★ **Setze *to be* in die richtige Kurzform.**

Mandy is telling her friend Barbara about Mark.

Mandy: I .... really cross with Mark. We .... often late for school because he never puts his things in the right place. He .... the most untidy person I know. Just imagine where he puts his shoes. They .... usually in the kitchen, but sometimes they .... even in the bathroom.

Barbara: But you .... not very tidy yourself. I .... still waiting for you to find the book you borrowed last year.

Mandy: But that .... Mark's fault. It .... somewhere under his bed with all the other things there.

Lösungen Seite 101

Alles klar?! Verwendung des *Simple Present*

	Das *simple present* verwendet man:
*I **go** to school by bike every day.*	für regelmäßige und gewohnheitsmäßige Handlungen
*The school **is** near my home.*	bei Tatsachenbeschreibungen
*The bike **belongs** to my brother.*	bei Zustandsverben
*I **often** eat cornflakes in the morning.*	Oft helfen Signalwörter bei der Entscheidung, ob man das ***simple present*** verwendet:

always ....

often ....

sometimes ....

never ....

every week ....

on Fridays ....

Ergänze die deutsche Übersetzung der Wörter. Diese Wörter solltest du dir gut merken.

Lernen mit System

Am besten schreibst du dir Sätze, die das *simple present* und Signalwörter enthalten, auf Klebezettel, die du in deinem Zimmer aufhängst, damit du sie immer wieder vor Augen hast. Eine andere Möglichkeit ist, dass du diese Sätze auf Karteikarten notierst und in deine Lernkartei einordnest, damit du sie oft wiederholst. So lernst du sie ganz automatisch. Überhaupt helfen dir Merkhilfen mit Klebezetteln oder Karteikarten, wenn du feststellst, dass du dir etwas schlecht merken kannst.

Lösungen Seite 101

Übung 4 **Setze die folgenden Verben in die richtige Form des *simple present.***

Katie always .... (to go) to school by bus. She .... (to like) to get to school early, so that she and her friends .... (to have) time to chat, before the bell .... (to ring) for the first lesson. Every week, her friend Anne .... (to tell) her what fun her riding lessons .... (to be) and Katie .... (to hope) that her next birthday present will be riding lessons, too. Anne .... (to say), "We often .... (to ride) across the fields and sometimes we even............................ (to jump) over fences if they .... (to be) not too high. My horse .... (to have) a lovely brown coat, which I always .... (to brush) after my lesson."

Lösungen Seite 102

2.2 *The Present Progressive*/Die Verlaufsform der Gegenwart

Alles klar?! **Bildung des *Present Progressive***

Ergänze die Lücken.

She is reading a magazine.

Das *present progressive* bildet man mit einer Form von *to be* und der *-ing*-Form (= Grundform des Verbs, z. B. *read* + *-ing*).

Singular	**Plural**
I am (I'm) reading	*we* ....
you are	*you* ....
he	*they* ....
she	
it is (it's) sleeping	

Beim Schreiben beachtet man besonders:

*write → I'm **writing** a letter.*

- Verben, die mit einem stummen *-e* enden: Hier entfällt das ....

*swim → She's **swimming**.*

- Verben mit kurzem, einfachem Vokal, auf den ein Konsonant folgt: Der Konsonant wird ....

*lie → He's **lying** in his bed.*

- Verben, die auf *-ie* enden: Das .... wird zu einem ....

Übung 1 **Suche das passende Verb aus der Liste aus und setze es ins *present progressive*.**

to look | to write | to read | to buy | to wait | to walk | to work | to eat

He .... in the garden.

She .... food in the supermarket.

You .... an apple.

They .... for the bus.

We .... to school.

You .... a book.

I .... an email.

He .... for his football boots.

Lösungen Seite 102

Alles klar?! **Verwendung des *Present Progressive***

Look! The children are playing in the garden.

***At the moment** Mary is throwing the ball.*

Das *present progressive* verwendet man:
für Handlungen, die gerade in diesem Moment stattfinden.

Oft helfen **Signalwörter** bei der Entscheidung, ob man das *present progressive* verwendet:

at the moment ....

now ....

just ....

Look! ....

Ergänze die deutsche Übersetzung der Wörter.
Diese Wörter solltest du dir gut merken.

Übung 2 **Setze die folgenden Verben ins *present progressive*.**

This afternoon Mark .... (to play) football at school.

He .... (to run) up and down the pitch. His team .... (to lead) by one goal. Their teacher calls out, "You .... (to do) well."

"I .... (to get) thirsty," Mark thinks. It is now half time.

The boys .... (to drink) orange juice and .... (to have) a short rest. Now the second half .... (to begin). The other team .... (to try) hard to score a goal. They .... (to pass) the ball from one player to another and .... (to wait) for a chance to shoot.

Now Mark .... (to shout) to the goalkeeper, "Look out, the ball .... (to come) towards you!" But it's too late, it's in the net.

At the moment Mark .... (to feel) cross.

"We .... (to play) badly," he shouts out.

But soon he .... (to kick) the ball towards the goal and in it goes. His team is the winner.

Lösungen Seite 102

2.3 *The Simple Past*/Die einfache Vergangenheit

Alles klar?! **Bildung des *Simple Past***

*They watch**ed** a film on TV last night.*	Beim ***simple past*** bei regelmäßigen Verben hängt man an die Grundform des Verbs .... an. *I play.........., you help.........., she call..........* Beim Schreiben beachtet man besonders:
*She hurr**ied** home.*	• Verben, die auf Mitlaut (Konsonant) + *y* enden: Das *y* wird zu ...., und man hängt .... an.
*She smil**ed** happily*	• Verben, die mit einem stummen *-e* enden: Hier entfällt das ....
*She pla**nn**ed the trip.*	• Verben mit kurzem, einfachem Vokal, auf den ein Konsonant folgt: Der Konsonant wird ....
*I **caught** the ball.*	Leider wird das *simple past* mancher Verben nicht regelmäßig gebildet. Diese Verben muss man lernen. *catch* → .... *write* → .... *do* → .... Wenn du das *simple past* der hier gesuchten Verben vergessen hast, sieh auf Seite 125/126 nach. Dort findest du eine Liste mit Verben, die du so lange üben solltest, bis du dir ganz sicher bist, wie die Formen lauten.

Lerntipp

Leider bleibt es dir nicht erspart, Formen wie die unregelmäßigen Verben zu lernen. Aber nicht immer kannst du alles wissen, manchmal hilft es dir weiter, wenn du weißt, wo du nachschauen kannst. Wenn du dir bei einer Hausaufgabe unsicher bist, wie eine Vergangenheitsform heißt, schau lieber nach. Denn auch dadurch prägst du dir die Formen ein, und vielleicht fällt sie dir dann in der nächsten Klassenarbeit ein.

Lösungen Seite 103

Übung 1 **Suche das passende Verb aus der Liste aus und setze es in die richtige Form von *simple past.***

to walk | to like | to play | to learn | to pass | to carry | to open | to plan

They .... home.

Mr Johnson .... the bag.

The teacher .... the window.

The class .... ten new verbs.

Mark .... football.

He .... the ball to the nearest player.

They .... their holiday.

Anne .... riding.

Übung 2 **Setze die unregelmäßigen Verben in die richtige Form von *simple past.***

1. Mark .... (to run) up and down the pitch.
2. Mark's team .... (to win) the match, but the other team .... (to lose).
3. They .... (to go) home by bus. He .... (to buy) eggs for breakfast.
4. Mark .... (to find) the book and .... (to give) it to Mandy.
5. He .... (to do) his homework in five minutes.
6. She .... (to see) a fox in the garden.
7. They .... (to drive) to the seaside by car.
8. The school choir .... (to sing) three songs.

Lösungen Seite 103

Alles klar?! Verwendung des *Simple Past*

My sister ***passed*** *her driving test last week.*	Das ***simple past*** verwendet man für abgeschlossene Ereignisse in der Vergangenheit.
	Oft helfen **Signalwörter** bei der Entscheidung, ob man das *simple past* verwendet:
I ***saw*** *her* ***yesterday****.*	*yesterday* ....
	last week ....
	two years ago ....
	Ergänze die deutsche Übersetzung. Diese Wörter solltest du dir gut merken.

Übung 3 ★ Setze die folgenden Verben in die richtige Form des *simple past.*

Last year Katie .... (to start) secondary school in the middle of Canterbury. All week before school .... (to begin), she .... (to worry) about her new life, but on the first morning she .... (to wake) up early and .... (to feel) fine. She .... (to leave) home in good time for the bus, which .... (to take) ten minutes to reach her school. She .... (to find) everything there very exciting and soon .... (to make) friends with two other pupils, Anne and Jane. She .... (to think) that the maths lesson .... (to be) boring, but she .... (to like) French very much. Her teacher, Mrs James, ... (to tell) the class that they .... (to be) all very good, but that Katie .... (to speak) French best of all.

Lösungen Seite 103

STOPP!
Zuerst die Lernkärtchen durcharbeiten!

Abschlusstest (20 Minuten)

Aufgabe 1 **Vervollständige die folgenden Sätze mit der richtigen Form von *to be*.**

a) The football match .... over.
b) We .... the winners.
c) I .... hungry.
d) Mark .... untidy.
e) Mandy .... cross.
f) They .... late.

Punkte: ☐ von 6

Aufgabe 2 **Suche das passende Verb aus und setze es ins *simple present*.**

to go | to put | to wait | to get | to hurry | to like

a) Every morning Mandy .... for Mark.
b) He always .... his school things in the wrong place.
c) They often .... to school late.
d) Katie sometimes .... to catch the bus.
e) I .... to chat with my friends every day.
f) Anne .... riding every Saturday.

Punkte: ☐ von 6

Aufgabe 3 **Setze die Verben in die richtige Form des *present progressive*.**

Katie .... (to have) a French lesson now. Mrs James .... (to teach) the class new words. At present the pupils .... (to talk) to each other and some .... (to laugh). Mrs James says to them, "Be quiet, please. You .... (to make) too much noise at the moment. I .... (to find) it very difficult to teach you anything today."

Punkte: ☐ von 6

Lösungen Seite 104

Aufgabe 4 **Setze die Verben in die richtige Form der Gegenwart (*simple present* oder *present progressive*).**

The twins .... (to feed: füttern) Maggie every day in the morning.

It is Monday morning and time to go to school. Mark is late again. He ....

(to put) Maggie's cat food into her dish now and Mandy .... (call) to him,

"Where are you? We must go." Now they .... (to hurry) to school and

Mark .... (to run) very fast. Mandy .... (to try) to run quickly, too.

"You .... (to go) too fast," Mandy says. But now the bell ....

(to ring) for the first lesson. Mark calls out, "Hurry up, you are so slow."

Punkte: ☐ von 8

Aufgabe 5 **Setze die folgenden Verben in die richtige Form des *simple past*.**

Last weekend Mandy .... (to stay) with her friend Barbara. It ....

(to be) Barbara's birthday and six school friends .... (to come) to her party.

First they .... (to play) games outside. They .... (to run) round the

garden playing 'hide-and-seek' (Verstecken). Then they .... (to eat) sausages and

.... (to drink) lemonade. In the evening they .... (to sing) songs and

Mandy .... (to play) her recorder (Blockflöte). When they .... (to go) to

bed, they soon .... (to fall) asleep.

Punkte: ☐ von 11

Punkte: ☐ von 35

30–35: Bravo! Du weißt über die Zeiten schon gut Bescheid.
20–30: Teilweise bist du sicher, teilweise noch nicht. Bearbeite bitte noch mal die Übungen, bei denen du beim ersten Mal viele Fehler hattest.
0–20: Leider ist dir noch zu vieles unklar. Arbeite das Kapitel bitte noch mal durch.

 Lösungen Seite 104

3

Satzformen

The Johnsons visit their grandparents in London. Mr and Mrs Booth, Bill and Mary, are Mrs Johnson's parents. Katie, Mandy and Mark love to visit their grandparents, who live in Wimbledon, a famous suburb of London. Wimbledon is some distance from the centre of London, but the children love to travel by Underground and when they visit their grandparents, there are always lots of things to see and do – go for a boat trip on the Thames, visit the Tower of London or feed the pigeons in Trafalgar Square.

3.1 *The Statement*/Der Aussagesatz

Alles klar?! *Positive Statement*/Bejahter Aussagesatz

The twins like picnics. S P O	Im Englischen gibt eine ganz einfache Formel, mit der man sich die Wortstellung merken kann. **S (Subjekt) – P (Prädikat) – O (Objekt)**
They go on a trip every Sunday.	Diese Wortstellung ändert sich auch nicht, wenn weitere Satzteile angehängt werden.

Alles klar?! *Negative Statement*/Verneinter Aussagesatz

*Today Katie **isn't (is not)** going with them.*	Bei der Verneinung wird ***not*** in Verbindung mit einem **Hilfsverb** gebraucht. In der gesprochenen Sprache wird hier oft die Kurzform verwendet: *he/she/it **is not*** — *he/she/it* .... *you/we/they **are not*** — *you/we/they* .... Bei der ersten Person Singular werden meist das Personalpronomen und das Hilfsverb zusammengezogen: ***I am not → I'm not***
*The twins **don't (do not)** like long queues.*	Ist in einem Satz kein **Hilfsverb** vorhanden, verwendet man das Hilfsverb ***to do***. Man spricht dann von der Umschreibung mit ***to do***. Dass die 3. Person Singular von ***to do*** unregelmäßig ist, ist schon bekannt: ***he/she/it does***.
*Katie **doesn't (does not)** like pigeons.*	Das ***-s*** bei der 3. Person Singular braucht man nur einmal. Es wird an ***to do*** angehängt: ***do → does***. Das Hauptverb steht in der Grundform. *Katie **likes** pigeons. → Katie **doesn't like** pigeons.*
*They **didn't (did not)** visit the Tower last year.* *They **didn't** go by car.*	Dass die Vergangenheitsform von ***do*** unregelmäßig ist, ist schon bekannt (***did***). Auch hier braucht man die „Anzeige", dass es Vergangenheit ist, nur einmal: Sie wandert vom Hauptverb auf das ***did***, das Hauptverb steht in der Grundform. *They **visited** the Tower last year. → They **didn't visit** the Tower last year.*

Lösungen Seite 105

Übung 1 **Verwandle die bejahten Aussagesätze in negative Aussagesätze.**

1. The twins visited the Tower of London.

....

2. Katie likes travelling by train.

....

3. The Booths live in Wimbledon.

....

4. Ben promised to take Mark to judo class.

....

5. Their grandparents took the twins to a tennis match.

....

6. Anne told Katie about her riding lessons.

....

Lerntipp
Nicht vergessen: Im Englischen brauchst du bei der Verneinung immer ein Hilfsverb.

The Tower of London

Lösungen Seite 105

Alles klar?! ***Verbs with two Objects*/Verben mit zwei Objekten**

The twins wrote Grandma Mary a postcard.

Manche Verben können zwei Objekte haben:

- ein Dativ- oder indirektes Objekt – Frage: **Wem?**
- ein Akkusativ- oder direktes Objekt – Frage: **Wen oder was?**

The twins wrote ***Grandma Mary a postcard*.**

....

Das indirekte Objekt steht .... dem direkten Objekt.

Weitere Verben:

to bring	....	*to read*	....
to buy	....	*to send*	....
to give	....	*to show*	....
to make	....	*to take*	....
to pay	....	*to tell*	....
to promise	....	*to write*	....

Übung 2 **Vervollständige die Sätze mit den folgenden direkten Objekten.**

recorder | apple | book | ball | car | horse | cat | goal

1. The sports teacher throws .... to Ben.
2. Mr Johnson washes .... every Saturday.
3. The twins play .... in the orchestra.
4. Mark and Mandy give .... its food every morning.
5. Katies brushes .... after her riding lesson.
6. Ben eats .... for lunch at school.
7. Mark scores .... in the football game.
8. Katie reads .... in the evening.

Lösungen Seite 105

Übung 3 **Trage die direkten und indirekten Objekte in Klammern in der richtigen Reihenfolge ein.**

1. The twins gave .... (the cat/its food).
2. Mr Johnson promised .... (a trip to London/the children).
3. Mrs Johnson wrote .... (a letter/her mother).
4. Katie showed .... (the email/Ann).
5. Mrs Johnson bought .... (the twins/an ice cream).
6. The twins sent .... (a postcard/their friend).
7. Grandma Mary made .... (the twins/a cake).
8. The teacher told .... (a story/the class).

Übung 4 ★ **Bilde Sätze mit jeweils einem direkten und einem indirekten Objekt.**

her friend | me | Mark | a story | an email | to the museum | a red dress | Katie | the children | a new mountain bike | the way to the Tower | Mandy | the twins a birthday cake | a letter | his class |

1. The policeman showed ....
2. Anne wrote ....
3. Mr and Mrs Johnson bought ....
4. Ben sent ....
5. Mother makes .... every year.
6. Grandma tells .... every evening.
7. The teacher took ....
8. My mother promised .... for Christmas.

Lösungen Seite 106

3.2 *Questions*/Fragen

Alles klar?! ***Yes/No Questions*/Ja-/Nein-Fragen**

- Bei der **Fragebildung** bleibt die schon bekannte Wortstellung **S – P – O** erhalten: Das Hauptverb folgt auf das Subjekt, nur das Hilfsverb wandert vor das Subjekt.

  The twins ***are feeding*** *the pigeons.*

  S **P** **O**

  Are *the twins* ***feeding*** *the pigeons?*

- Wie bei der Verneinung wird auch bei der Fragebildung die Umschreibung mit **to do** benötigt, wenn kein anderes Hilfsverb im Satz vorhanden ist. Hierdurch bleibt die Wortstellung **S – P – O** auch im Fragesatz erhalten.

  The twins ***like*** *picnics.*

  S **P** **O**

  Do *the twins* ***like*** *picnics?*

- Wie bei der Verneinung braucht man das **–s** der dritten Person Singular nur einmal. Es wird an ***to do*** angehängt: ***do*** → ***does***. Das Hauptverb steht in der Grundform.

  Katie ***likes*** *pigeons.*

  S **P** **O**

  Does *Katie* ***like*** *pigeons?*

- Wie bei der Verneinung braucht man die „Anzeige" für die Vergangenheit nur einmal. Sie wandert vom Hauptverb auf das ***did***, das Hauptverb steht in der Grundform.

  They ***visited*** *the Tower last year.*

  S **P** **O**

  Did *they* ***visit*** *the Tower last year?*

Übung 1 **Forme die Aussagesätze in Fragen um.**

1. Mrs Johnson works for the church.

....

2. They went to London by car.

....

Lösungen Seite 106

3. The twins are watching the Changing of the Guard.

....

4. They visited Buckingham Palace last year.

....

5. Maggie likes to catch mice.

....

6. The twins like playing the recorder.

....

Alles klar?! ***Short Answers*/Kurzantworten**

Are *the twins feeding the pigeons?*
- *Yes,* ***they are****.*
- *No,* ***they aren't****.*

Do *the twins like picnics?*
- *Yes,* ***they do****.*
- *No,* ***they don't****.*

Does *she like pigeons?*
- *Yes,* ***she does****.*
- *No,* ***she doesn't****.*

Did *they go by car?*
- *Yes,* ***they did****.*
- *No,* ***they didn't****.*

Wenn Ja-/Nein-Fragen beantwortet werden, verwendet man **Kurzantworten**, d. h., man wiederholt in der Antwort Subjekt und (verneintes) Hilfsverb.

Ein einfaches ***Yes*** oder ***No*** reicht im Englischen nicht aus – es wird als ziemlich unhöflich empfunden.

Übung 2 **Ergänze die Sätze mit der richtigen Kurzantwort.**

1. Does Anne like riding? Yes, ...
2. Did Mark go to judo? No, ...
3. Are the guards at the Tower called Beefeaters? Yes, ...
4. Did the Johnsons go to London by car? Yes, ...
5. Do the twins have inline skates? No, ...
6. Does Ben have a horse? No, ...

Lösungen Seite 106

Alles klar?! *Wh-Questions*/Fragen mit Fragewort

Where *are the twins going on Sunday?* ***When*** *does the boat leave?* ***What*** *do they have for lunch on their trips?* ***How*** *do they usually go?*	Neben Entscheidungsfragen gibt es Fragen mit Fragewort. Die wichtigsten Fragewörter sind: *who?* .... *which?* .... *where?* .... *when?* .... *why?* .... *what?* .... *how?* .... *whose?* ....
Whose *bag is that?* ***Why*** *did Katie stay at home?*	Auch bei den meisten Fragen mit Fragewort braucht man ein Hilfsverb, damit die Wortstellung **S – P – O** erhalten bleibt. *They* ***have*** *sandwiches for lunch ...* **S P O** ***What do*** *they* ***have*** *for lunch?*
Who *likes picnics?* ***Which*** *boat leaves earlier?* ***Who*** *stayed at home*	Mit ***who*** und ***which*** (+ Nomen) fragt man nach dem Subjekt. Hier wird das Hilfsverb nicht vorgezogen, bzw. man braucht keine Umschreibung mit ***to do***. Wenn du die Satzglieder unter die Sätze schreibst, wird klar, warum das so ist. ***Who*** *likes picnics?* .... Weil man bei ***who*** nicht weiß, wie viele Subjekte beteiligt sind, steht das Verb (im Präsens) in der **3. Person Singular**.

Lerntipp

Who (wer) und **Where** (wo) sind zwei Wörter, die wir als Deutsche manchmal verwechseln. Wenn dir das auch schon mal passiert ist, kannst du dir einen Klebezettel oder ein Lernkärtchen mit zwei Sätzen schreiben, die dir die Bedeutung zeigen, und vielleicht ein kleines Bild dazu zeichnen, z. B.:

Who is Mark? **Where** does he live?

Lösungen Seite 107

Alles klar?! ***How many* und *How much***

How many *sandwiches have we got?*	Mit ***how many*** fragt man nach zählbaren Nomen.
How much *milk is left?*	Mit ***how much*** fragt man nach nichtzählbaren Nomen, d.h. Nomen, die du nicht in den Plural setzen kannst. (→ Kap. 1, Seite 7)

Übung 3 **Bilde Fragen mit den Fragewörtern *who, how much, how many, where, why, what*. In den unterstrichenen Satzteilen steht, wonach du fragen sollst.**

1. The Johnsons live <u>in Charlton Road, Canterbury</u>.

   ....

2. The train for London leaves <u>at 10.30</u>.

   ....

3. The Johnsons' house has <u>eight windows</u>.

   ....

4. <u>Mary</u> is riding Anne's horse.

   ....

5. The twins have <u>sandwiches and apples</u> for their picnic.

   ....

6. There are <u>two centimetres</u> of milk left in the glass.

   ....

7. Katie stayed at home <u>because she was tired</u>.

   ....

8. The church bell rings <u>at six o'clock in the evening</u>.

   ....

9. Maggie is sleeping <u>in her basket</u>.

   ....

10. <u>The Booths</u> live in Wimbledon.

   ....

Lösungen Seite 107

3.3 *Imperatives*/Befehlsform

Alles klar?! Imperatives/Befehlsform

Hurry up, *we are late.* ***Look****, the Tower is over there.*	Mit der Befehlsform drückt man einen Befehl, eine Aufforderung, eine Bitte aus. Im Englischen gibt es dafür nur eine Form für Singular wie für Plural: die Grundform des Verbs ohne *to*. **Singular** / **Plural** ***Hurry up.*** → *Beeil dich!* / *Beeilt euch!* Bei der Befehlsform steht im Englischen kein Ausrufezeichen.
Don't go *too close to the water.*	Bei der Verneinung wird ***do not*** oder ***don't*** dem Verb vorangestellt.
Let's go *now.*	Wenn eine Aufforderung, ein Vorschlag oder eine Bitte den Sprechenden mit einschließt, verwendet man ***Let us*** oder ***Let's***.

Übung 1 Setze die folgenden Verben in die Befehlsform.

1. You are late for school, Mark. .... (to hurry) up.
2. We are tired. .... (to go) home.
3. (Mark to his father) "I kicked the ball through the window. .... (not to be) angry."
4. (Mr Johnson to Mark) "Next time .... (to be) more careful."

Lösungen Seite 107

3.4 *Subordinate Clauses*/Nebensätze

Alles klar?! ***Subordinate Clauses*/Nebensätze**

Katie doesn't go to the Tower ***because*** *she wants to go to a birthday party.*

Auch in Nebensätzen gilt die Wortstellung **S – P – O**. Weitere Wörter, mit denen man Haupt- und Nebensätze verbinden kann:

before ....

but ....

when ....

Übung 1 **Übersetze die unterstrichenen Satzteile**

1. Die Zwillinge wollen eine Bootsfahrt auf der Themes machen, <u>weil das Wetter schön (fine) ist.</u>

   ....

2. <u>Bevor die Johnsons die U-Bahn nehmen</u>, müssen sie Einkäufe für die Großeltern machen.

   ....

3. <u>Als sie das Boot erreichen</u>, fängt es zu regnen an.

   ....

4. Die Zwillinge sind unglücklich, <u>weil sie den Ausflug nicht machen</u> (to go on the trip).

   ....

Lösungen Seite 107

STOPP!
Zuerst die Lernkärtchen durcharbeiten!

Abschlusstest (25 Minuten)

Aufgabe 1 **Ändere die Aussagesätze jeweils in das Gegenteil.**

a) Katie is doing her French homework in her room.

....

b) The Booths don't live in Wimbledon.

....

c) Mandy sent Anne an email.

....

d) The twins have got a television in their room.

....

e) Anne does not brush her horse every day.

....

f) The Johnsons did not have a picnic in the park.

....

Punkte: ☐ von 6

Aufgabe 2 **Bens Freund Danny aus London wird für die Schulzeitschrift interviewt. Stelle die Fragen.**

a) .... Canterbury?

No, I don't. I come from London.

b) .... parents ....?

Yes, they do, but they were born in Ireland.

c) .... friend ....?

No, he doesn't live in Charlton Rd.

d) .... you and Ben ....?

Yes, we did. We met at the judo club.

Lösungen Seite 108

e) ....?

Yes, I really like it, it is a cool sport.

f) .... subjects at school?

No, I don't. I don't like maths.

Punkte: ☐ von 6

Aufgabe 3 **Frage nach den unterstrichenen Wörtern mit *who, what, where, when, why*.**

a) Anne has a riding lesson every Saturday.

....

b) Katie is reading her French textbook.

....

c) The twins play football in the garden.

....

d) Mr Johnson owns a car.

....

e) We went to the Tower of London last week.

....

f) Ben's birthday is in May.

....

g) The Johnson's house is in Charlton Road.

....

h) The twins like inline skating because it is fun.

....

i) The Beefeaters guard the Tower of London.

....

j) We are going to school by bus today, because it is raining.

....

Punkte: ☐ von 10

Lösungen Seite 108

Aufgabe 4 **Übersetze ins Englische.**

a) Katies Mutter schrieb einen Brief an die Lehrerin.

....

b) Mutter versprach mir ein neues Kleid zu Weihnachten.

....

c) Der Lehrer nahm die Kinder ins Museum mit.

....

d) Der Polizist zeigte ihnen den Weg zum Tower.

....

Punkte: ☐ von 8

Aufgabe 5 **Die Wörter der Nebensätze stehen in der falschen Reihenfolge. Schreibe sie richtig auf. Unterstreiche die Befehlsformen.**

a) When you the Tower of London visit, look out for the ravens.

....

b) Their wings are clipped (= Ihre Flügel sind gestutzt) because they in the Tower stay must.

....

c) When you the Crown Juwels (= Kronjuwelen) see, don't miss the Koh-i-Noor diamond.

....

d) It is famous because it one of the largest diamonds in the world is.

....

Punkte: ☐ von 4

Punkte: ☐ von 34

30–34: Bravo! Du weißt über den Satzbau schon gut Bescheid.
19–29: Teilweise bist du sicher, teilweise noch nicht. Bearbeite bitte noch einmal die Übungen, in denen du beim ersten Mal viele Fehler hattest.
0–18: Leider ist dir noch zu vieles unklar. Arbeite das Kapitel bitte noch mal durch.

Lösungen Seite 108

4

Zahlen, Uhrzeit, Datum

Katie wants to learn to ride. It is her birthday soon and she hopes that her parents will give her riding lessons as a present. Her friend Anne already has lessons and Katie wants to go to the same riding school. The twins play the recorder in the school orchestra. In their free time they enjoy different sports. Mandy has a monocycle and Mark likes inline skating. They are both members of a judo club.

4.1 *Numbers*/Zahlen

Alles klar?! ***The Cardinal Numbers*/Die Grundzahlen**

*There are **eleven** players in a football team.*	Mit Grundzahlen werden Dinge oder Lebewesen gezählt. Folgende Zahlen kannst du sicher schon ohne Probleme schreiben. 1 .... 6 .... 11 .... 16 .... 2 .... 7 .... 12 .... 17 .... 3 .... 8 .... 13 .... 18 .... 4 .... 9 .... 14 .... 19 .... 5 .... 10 .... 15 .... 20 ....
*There are **twenty-five** children in the school orchestra.*	Bei Zahlen, die aus Zehner- und Einerzahl zusammengesetzt sind, steht, anders als im Deutschen, die Zehnerzahl **vor** der Einerzahl. Sie werden mit **Bindestrich** geschrieben. Zähle weiter: *twenty-one,* ...., ..., ...
thirteen children *thirty horses*	Bei den Zahlen mit *-teen* liegt die Hauptbetonung auf der zweiten Silbe, bei den Zahlen mit *-ty* auf der ersten.
*There are **two hundred and thirty-five** children in Mark and Mandy's school.* ***Fifty-seven thousand seven hundred and thirty-six** people live in Wimbledon.*	**Zahlen über 100** werden mit ***and*** verbunden. *A hundred/one hundred* und *a thousand/one thousand* werden immer mit unbestimmtem Artikel oder einer Zahlenangabe verwendet.
1,500 = one thousand five hundred *1,000,000 = a/one million* *1,000,000,000 = a/one billion*	**Bei Zahlen ab 1000** wird zur besseren Lesbarkeit nach drei Stellen ein Komma gesetzt (außer bei Jahreszahlen). Eine Milliarde heißt auf Englisch ***billion***.
It's zero degrees (0°C). *The Johnson's phone number is 3650191.*	Für die **Null** gibt es auf Englisch zwei Bezeichnungen: • Beim Rechnen und bei Maßangaben (z. B. Temperatur) heißt die Null **zero**. • Bei Telefonnummern spricht man die Null wie ein **„O"** [əʊ].

Lösungen Seite 109

Übung 1

Schreibe die Zahlen in Worten auf.

Today is March 15th. It is Katie's birthday. She is (14) .... She has a lot of presents. She has (4) .... books, (3) .... CDs, (2) .... pairs of trousers and (18) .... birthday cards. In one of them is a voucher (= Gutschein) for (10) .... riding lessons. She is very happy now. At her party Mark and Mandy play (6) .... of Katie's favourite tunes (= Lieblingsmelodien) on their recorders. They also give her (3) .... pictures of Maggie, which they painted themselves. And what did Maggie give her? (1) .... dead mouse, of course.

Lerntipp

Auf Englisch gibt es Merkverse, mit denen du die Zahlen üben kannst:

One, two, three, four, five*, once I caught a fish alive.*
Six, seven, eight, nine, ten*, then I let it go again.*

There are ***ten*** *green bottles sitting on the wall,*
ten *green bottles sitting on the wall.*
And if ***one*** *green bottle should accidentally fall,*
there'll be ***nine*** *green bottles sitting on the wall.*
Nine *green bottles …*

Lösungen Seite 109

Übung 2 **Beantworte die Fragen mit der richtigen Zahl.**

1. How many months does a year have? ....
2. How many days does a week have? ....
3. How many hours are there in a day? ....
4. How many minutes are there in an hour? ....
5. How many days does March have? ....
6. How many legs does an insect have? ....
7. How many rings does the Olympic flag have? ....
8. How many days are there in a year? ....

Übung 3 ★ **Mandy und Mark haben vier neue Freunde im Judoclub gefunden. Leider haben sie ihre Telefonnummern falsch aufgeschrieben. Kannst du die Fehler finden?**

1. 8596071 eight – five – six – nine – 0 – seven – one ....
2. 7934512 seven – nine – five – four – three – one – two ....
3. 4848625 four – eight – four – eight – two – six – five ....
4. 1096745 one – zero – nine – six – seven – four – five ....

Lösungen Seite 109

Alles klar?! ***The Ordinal Numbers*/Die Ordnungszahlen**

*Today is Mark's **first (1st)** big football match.*

*Mark plays the **second (2nd)** recorder in the school orchestra.*

*This is the **third (3rd)** time that the twins are late for school this week.*

Eine Reihenfolge wird mit **Ordnungszahlen** angegeben. Wenn sie als Ziffern geschrieben werden, stellt man die letzten beiden Buchstaben hinter der Zahl hoch.

Die ersten drei Ordnungszahlen lauten:
first → 1st, second → 2nd, third → 3rd.

Ab der Zahl *four* werden sie mit der Endung ***-th*** gebildet, die an die Grundzahl angehängt wird:
fourth (4th), thirteenth (13th), twenty-sixth (26th), one hundredth (100th), …

Besondere Schreibungen: *five → fifth (5th), eight → eighth (8th), nine → ninth (9th), twelve → twelfth (12th), twenty → twentieth (20th)*

Übung 4 **Wenn du die richtigen Buchstaben aufschreibst, weißt du, was sich Mark zum Geburtstag wünscht.**

1. The first letter of the time of year, when everyone gives and gets presents. ☐
2. The second letter of the capital (= Hauptstadt) of England. ☐
3. The third letter of the famous London suburb where Katie's grandparents live. ☐
4. The first letter of the capital of France. ☐
5. The second letter of the sports club, where Mark and Mandy are members. ☐
6. The fourth letter of the town, where the Johnsons live. ☐
7. The second letter of the capital of Germany. ☐
8. The third letter of the country where you live. ☐

Lösungen Seite 109

4.2 *Time*/Uhrzeit

Alles klar?! **So nennst du die Uhrzeit**

What's the time, please?

Can you tell me the time, please?

… sind die beiden Fragen, mit denen man nach der Uhrzeit fragt.

It's two o'clock.
a quarter ***past*** *two.*
twenty ***past*** *two.*
half past *two.*
a quarter to *three.*
five ***to*** *three.*

two o'clock

a quarter ***past*** *two*

a quarter ***to*** *three*

Für Uhrzeiten zwischen der vollen und der halben Stunde verwendet man ***past*** (nach), ab der 31. Minute ***to*** (vor).

School starts at ***9 am****.*

Katie's riding lesson starts at ***5 pm****.*

The telephone rang at **5.30 in the morning***!*

Im Englischen unterteilt man den Tag in der Regel in zwei Hälften: Die Stunden von Mitternacht bis zum Mittag erhalten den Zusatz ***am*** (von lat. ante meridiem – vor dem Mittag), der Nachmittag und Abend bis Mitternacht den Zusatz ***pm*** (von lat. post meridiem – nach dem Mittag).

Wenn man bei Uhrzeiten zwischen den Stunden deutlich machen will, ob Vor- oder Nachmittag gemeint ist, kann man folgende Zusätze ergänzen:

in the morning ....

in the afternoon ....

in the evening ....

at night ....

The train leaves at ***14.35 (= fourteen thirty-five).***

It's ***2.15 (= two fifteen)****.*

Bei Fahrplänen verwendet man auf Englisch inzwischen immer öfter auch die 24-Stunden-Uhr, um die Ankunfts- und Abfahrtszeiten anzusagen.

Mögliche Antworten auf die Frage, wie spät es ist:
It's exactly … (wenn man es ganz genau weiß)
It's about … (wenn man es nur ungefähr weiß)
I'm sorry, I haven't got a watch. I don't know (wenn man es nicht weiß).

Lösungen Seite 110

Übung 1 **Schreibe die folgenden Uhrzeiten auf.**

a)...................... b)......................... c)......................... d) ....

e)...................... f)......................... g) .... h) ....

Übung 2 **Ordne die richtigen Begriffe zu.**

alarm clock | church clock | grandfather clock | pocket watch | wrist watch

a) .... b) ....

c) .... d) .... e) ....

Lösungen Seite 110

Übung 3 ★ **Schau dir den Stundenplan von Mandy und Mark an und schreibe die Uhrzeiten auf.**

	Monday	Tuesday	Wednesday	Thursday	Friday
9.00–12.30	Lessons	Lessons	Lessons	Lessons	Lessons
12.30–14.00	Lunch	Lunch	Lunch	Lunch	Lunch
14.00–16.00	Lessons	Lessons	Lessons	Lessons	Lessons
16.00–16.30	Break		Break	Break	
16.30–17.00	Football practice		Orchestra Practice	Football practice	
17.00–18.00					
18.00–19.00					Judo Club

1. When does school start? At ....
2. When does Mandy and Mark's lunch break start? At ....
3. When does school begin in the afternoon? At ....
4. When does football practice start? At ....
5. When does Mandy go home on Monday and Thursday? At ....
6. When does orchestra practice begin? At ....
7. When do Mandy and Mark go home on Wednesday? At ....
8. When do Mandy and Mark go to the Judo club? At ....

Nursery Rhyme

Hickory Dickory Dock
The mouse ran up the clock
The clock struck one
The mouse ran down
Hickory Dickory Dock

Lösungen Seite 110

4.3 *Dates*/Datumsangaben

Alles klar?! **Schreibweisen des Datums**

The twin's birthday is on ***May 25th/25th May.***	Bei Datumsangaben kann man den Monatsnamen an erste oder an zweite Stelle schreiben. Gesprochen wird das Datum wie folgt: *May 25th → May the twenty-fifth* *25th May → the twenty-fifth of May*
25/05/2008 (GB) *05/25/2008 (USA)*	Wenn man ein Datum nur mit Ziffern schreibt, gibt es in Großbritannnien (GB) und den USA unterschiedliche Reihenfolgen. Unter Umständen kann das zu Missverständnissen führen. Was bedeutet folgendes Datum? **GB** **USA** **08/05/2008** ....
The football match is ***on Saturday****.*	Die **Namen** der Wochentage ***(days of the week)*** lauten: *Monday, Tuesday, Wednesday, Thursday, Friday, Saturday, Sunday*
Katie's birthday is ***in March****.*	Die **Namen** der Monate ***(months)*** lauten: *January, February, March, April, May, June, July, August, September, Oktober, November, December* Die **Namen** der ***Wochentage*** und ***Monate*** werden immer ***großgeschrieben***.

Lösungen Seite 110

Übung 1 **Schreibe die folgenden Datumsangaben auf.**
Beispiel: 17.5.1972 – 17th May 1972 oder May 17th 1972.

1. 29.12.2007 ....
2. 7.8.2001 ....
3. 11.11.1996 ....
4. 3.6.1999 ....
5. 12.1.2000 ....
6. 15.7.1982 ....
7. 22.10.2002 ....
8. 9.4.2003 ....

Übung 2 **Wie spricht man die folgenden Datumsangaben? Schreibe auf.**

1. March 5th ....
2. August 2nd ....
3. 27th February ....
4. June 16th ....
5. November 4th ....
6. 25th September ....
7. January 3rd ....
8. 1st December ....

Merkverse
Thirty days has September, April, June, and November.
All the rest have thirty-one, except for February alone,
Which has twenty-eight days clear, and twenty-nine in each leap year.

Lösungen Seite 111

STOPP!
Zuerst die Lernkärtchen durcharbeiten!

Abschlusstest (25 Minuten)

Aufgabe 1 **Schreibe die Zahlen in Wörtern auf.**

a) 22: ....
b) 15: ....
c) 74: ....
d) 42: ....
e) 55: ....
f) 96: ....
g) 111: ....
h) 89: ....
i) 12: ....
j) 247: ....

Punkte: ☐ von 10

Aufgabe 2 **Wenn du die richtigen Buchstaben aufschreibst, erfährst du den Namen von Katies Pferd.**

☐ ☐ ☐ ☐ ☐ ☐   ☐ ☐ ☐ ☐ ☐ ☐ ☐

1. The twelfth letter of the alphabet.
2. The ninth letter of the alphabet.
3. The twentieth letter of the alphabet.
4. The twentieth letter of the alphabet.
5. The twelfth letter of the alphabet.
6. The fifth letter of the alphabet.
7. The eighteenth letter of the alphabet.
8. The ninth letter of the alphabet.
9. The third letter of the alphabet.
10. The eighth letter of the alphabet.
11. The first letter of the alphabet.
12. The eighteenth letter of the alphabet.
13. The fourth letter of the alphabet.

Punkte: ☐ von 13

Aufgabe 3 **Wie spät ist es? Schreibe die folgenden Uhrzeiten auf und gib auch die Tageszeit *(in the morning/in the afternoon/in the evening/at night)* an.**

1. (18.30) It's ....
2. (13.20) It's ....
3. (9.45) It's ....
4. (4.55) It's ....
5. (16.25) It's ....
6. (19.00) It's ....
7. (1.05) It's ....
8. (6.50) It's ....

Punkte: ☐ von 8

Lösungen Seite 111

Aufgabe 4 **Schau dir noch einmal den Stundenplan von Mandy und Mark auf Seite 52 an und beantworte die folgenden Fragen zu den Wochentagen.**

1. On which day of the week do Mandy and Mark have orchestra practice?

On ....

2. On which days of the week does Mark have football practice?

On ....

3. On which day of the week do Mark and Mandy go to the Judo club?

On ....

4. On which day of the week do both twins go home at 4 o'clock?

On ....

Punkte: ☐ von 4

Aufgabe 5 **Katies neue Brieffreundin Julia aus Deutschland schreibt Katie eine E-Mail, in der sie ihr die Geburtstage in ihrer Familie mitteilt. Sie hat einige Fehler gemacht. Kannst du sie korrigieren? (Das richtige Datum ist in Klammern gesetzt.)**

Hi Katie,

You wanted to know, when our birthdays are. My father's birthday is on September 10th .... (10.10.). My mother's birthday is on 4th January .... (4.1.). My brother's birthday is on July 3rd .... (7.3.). My birthday is on August 15th .... (15.8.), when I hope to get lots of presents.

Hope to hear from you soon,

Julia

Punkte: ☐ von 4

Punkte: ☐ von 39

35–39: Bravo! Du weißt über die Zahlen, Daten und Zeiten schon gut Bescheid.
24–34: Teilweise bist du sicher, teilweise noch nicht. Bearbeite bitte noch einmal die Übungen, in denen du beim ersten Mal viele Fehler hattest.
0–24: Leider ist dir noch zu vieles unklar. Arbeite das Kapitel bitte noch mal durch.

Lösungen Seite 111/112

5 Angaben zu Ort, Zeit, Häufigkeit

Canterbury is not far from the coast, the nearest seaside resort is Dover, famous for its white cliffs. These are the first things a visitor sees when arriving at Dover Harbour by ferry from the continental mainland. There are, of course, other resorts along the coast, places such as Folkestone or Broadstairs, where the people of London often go for a day trip.

5.1 *Adverbial Phrases of Place*/Ortsangaben

Alles klar?! **Zusätzliche Informationen im Satz: Ortsangaben**

The Booths live ***in Wimbledon****.*

The Johnsons are on their way ***to Wimbledon***

Ortsangaben geben, wie der Name schon sagt, den Ort an, **wo** etwas stattfindet, oder eine Richtung (**wohin, woher**).

Ortsangaben stehen am Ende des Satzes.

The Booths live ***in Wimbledon****.*

S **P** **Ortsangabe**

Zauberformel

Erinnert ihr euch noch an die Zauberformel für die Satzstellung im Englischen: **S – P – O**? Sie hilft euch in diesem Kapitel wieder, wenn ihr in euren Sätzen zusätzliche Informationen, z. B. zu Ort, Zeit oder Häufigkeit, geben wollt.

Übung 1 **Beantworte die Fragen auf Englisch.**

1. Wo wohnen Katies Großeltern?

   ....

2. Wo spielen die Zwillinge Fußball?

   ....

3. Wo arbeitet Mrs Johnson?

   ....

4. Wo schläft Maggie?

   ....

Lösungen Seite 112

5.2 *Adverbial Phrases of Time/Zeitangaben*

Alles klar?! **Zusätzliche Informationen im Satz: Zeitangaben**

*The Johnsons leave the house **early in the morning**.* *The trip takes **one hour**.*	Zeitangaben informieren, wie der Name schon sagt, darüber, **wann** etwas stattfindet oder **wie lange** es dauert. Zeitangaben stehen in der Regel am Ende des Satzes. *The trip takes **one hour**.* ↓ S ↓ P ↓ Zeitangabe
***On Sundays** they visit their grandparents.*	Wenn man die Zeitangabe besonders betonen will, kann man sie auch an den Anfang des Satzes ziehen. Die Wortstellung S – P – O bleibt aber dennoch erhalten. ***On Sundays** they visit their grandparents.* ↓ Zeitangabe ↓ **S** ↓ **P** ↓ **O**

Übung 1 **Where/when? Bilde Sätze und beachte die Wortstellung im Englischen**

Beispiel: *starts / school / at 9 am / in England.*
School starts at 9 am in England.

1. go to primary school / the twins / in Canterbury / every day.

   ....

2. start secondary school / British pupils / when they are eleven.

   ....

3. a school uniform / Katie / at her school / must wear.

   ....

4. lunch / the twins / at school / can have.

   ....

5. at school / has / Katie / her music lesson.

   ....

6. her riding lesson / Ann / has / every Saturday / at the riding school.

   ....

Lösungen Seite 112

Dover Castle

Übung 2 ★ **Übersetze ins Englische.**

1. Mr Johnson geht frühmorgens ins Büro.

....

2. Die Familie macht heute einen Ausflug nach Dover.

....

3. Die Fahrt (journey) nach Dover dauert eine Stunde.

....

4. Die Besichtigung von (visit to) Dover Castle ist am Nachmittag.

....

5. Sonntags besuchen die Johnsons ihre Großeltern.

....

6. Die Zwillinge spielen dienstags im Schulorchester Blockflöte.

....

Lösungen Seite 112

Übung 3 **Setze die Satzteile in die richtige Reihenfolge.**

1. The Johnson twins/go/in Canterbury/to junior school.

   ....

2. Katie wants to visit/at the weekend/her friend/in Broadstairs.

   ....

3. Mark sees/every morning/Ben/at the bus stop.

   ....

4. The twins/have/a recorder lesson/every day/at school.

   ....

5. Katie/to her riding lesson/after school/goes.

   ....

6. The Johnsons are visiting/in Dover/on Saturday/the castle.

   ....

Lerntipp

Wenn du sowohl eine Ortsangabe als auch eine Zeitangabe hast, dann kommt die Ortsangabe vor der Zeitangabe – oder Place vor Time. Merken kannst du dir das nach der alphabetischen Reihenfolge der Anfangsbuchstaben (O–Z bzw. P–T).

The Johnsons go ***to Wimbledon every month.***
Wohin? (Ort) Wann? (Zeit)

The white cliffs of Dover

Lösungen Seite 112

5.3 *Adverbial Phrases of Frequency*/Häufigkeitsangaben

Alles klar?! **Zusätzliche Informationen im Satz: Häufigkeitsangaben**

*The Johnsons **often** visit Mrs Johnson's parents.*

Häufigkeitsangaben geben an, **wie oft** etwas geschieht.

The Johnsons	***often***	*visit*	*Mrs Johnson's parents.*
↓	↓	↓	↓
S	Häufigkeitsadverb	**P**	**O**

Erinnerst du dich? Die Häufigkeitsadverbien sind dir schon als Signalwörter für die Verwendung der einfachen Gegenwart begegnet. Bringe die folgenden Häufigkeitsadverbien in die richtige Reihenfolge. Beginne mit dem Adverb, das die geringste Häufigkeit angibt.

always *never* *often* *sometimes* *usually*

....

Übung 1 **Wie schreibt man das Adverb richtig?**

mseeosmti lysawa vreen tnoef llysuau

....

Übung 2 **Setze das Häufigkeitsadverb aus der Klammer an die richtige Stelle.**

1. (sometimes) Katie forgets her French homework.

   ....

2. (often) The Johnsons visit Mrs Johnson's parents in London.

   ....

3. (never) The twins go to school by bus.

   ....

4. (usually) Mrs Johnson works in the church office.

   ....

5. (sometimes) Ben and Mark go to the judo club on Tuesday.

   ....

6. (always) Maggie sleeps in her basket.

   ....

Lösungen Seite 113

STOPP!
Zuerst die Lernkärtchen durcharbeiten!

Abschlusstest (15 Minuten)

Aufgabe 1 **Schreibe diese Adverbien auf Englisch.**

a) manchmal ....

b) nie ....

c) immer ....

d) gewöhnlich ....

e) häufig ....

Punkte: ☐ von 5

Aufgabe 2 **Setze das Häufigkeitsadverb an die richtige Stelle.**

a) We go usually to school by bike.

....

b) The Johnsons spend the weekend in Broadstairs often.

....

c) Katie and the twins visit their grandparents sometimes together.

....

d) Always Mrs Johnson does the shopping at the supermarket.

....

e) Anne forgets never to brush her horse after riding.

....

f) Mr Johnson leaves the office usually at 5 pm.

....

Punkte: ☐ von 6

Lösungen Seite 113

Aufgabe 3 **Setze die Satzteile in die richtige Reihenfolge.**

a) The school bus/the bus stop/at 8 o'clock/leaves/usually.

....

b) At 10 am/always/Katie and Anne/go riding/on Saturdays.

....

c) In summer/often/the children/in the open-air pool/go swimming/at the beach.

....

d) Katie/her homework/does/at the table/never/in the dining-room.

....

e) Travels/the French teacher/sometimes/to Paris/in summer/in France.

....

f) Mr and Mrs Johnson/to the cinema/at the weekend/go/often.

....

Punkte: ☐ von 6

Punkte: ☐ von 17

14–17: Bravo! Du weißt über die Angaben zu Ort und Zeit schon gut Bescheid.
8–13: Teilweise bist du sicher, teilweise noch nicht. Bearbeite bitte noch einmal die Übungen, in denen du beim ersten Mal viele Fehler hattest.
0–7: Leider ist dir noch zu vieles unklar. Arbeite das Kapitel bitte noch mal durch.

Lösungen Seite 113

6

Präpositionen

Katie and the twins' other grandparents live in York, a historical walled city in the North of England, which has one of the largest Gothic cathedrals in Europe. It also has a very famous Railway Museum. York is situated near some beautiful countryside; one area of which is called the Yorkshire Dales with lovely hills and valleys. It is here that the Johnson's cousins, Jamie (14) and Matthew (10), live with their parents. All the Johnsons are meeting at their grandparents' house this weekend.

6.1 *Prepositions of Time*/Präpositionen der Zeit

Alles klar?! **So verwendet man *Prepositions of Time***

The museum opens ***at*** *ten o'clock.*

Eine **Präposition** steht meist vor dem Nomen oder Pronomen, daher auch ihr Name (lateinisch von prae = vor, ponere = stellen). Präpositionen legen das Verhältnis dieses Worts zum Rest des Satzes fest.

The museum opens ***at*** *ten o'clock.* *The Johnsons arrive there* ***in*** *the morning.*	Präpositionen der Zeit legen ein zeitliches Verhältnis fest: Man kann mit ihnen sagen, **wann** oder **wie lange** etwas geschieht.
in *(the year) 2000* ***in*** *spring, summer, autumn, winter* ***in*** *January, February, March, ...* ***in*** *the morning,* ***in*** *the afternoon,* ***in*** *the evening*	Wenn man von längeren Zeitabschnitten spricht, z. B. Jahren, Jahreszeiten, Monaten, Tageszeiten, verwendet man ***in***. Eine Ausnahme: ***at*** *night* = nachts
on *Monday, Tuesday, ...* ***on*** *June 1st*	Wenn man von Wochentagen spricht oder Datumsangaben macht, verwendet man ***on***.
at *ten o'clock* ***at*** *breakfast, lunch, tea* ***at*** *Easter, Christmas* ***at*** *the weekend* ***at*** *the same time*	Wenn man von bestimmten Zeitpunkten spricht, z. B. von Uhrzeiten, Mahlzeiten, Festtagen, verwendet man ***at***.
The Johnsons saw many trains ***before*** *lunch.* *They were very tired* ***after*** *their visit.* *They saw a lot of trains* ***during*** *their visit.* *They stayed there* ***until*** *four o'clock.* *They stayed there* ***between*** *ten and four o'clock.* *They stayed there* ***from*** *ten* ***until/to*** *four o'clock.*	Weitere wichtige Präpositionen der Zeit sind: *before* .... *after* .... *during* .... *until* .... *between* .... *from ... until/to* ....

Lösungen Seite 114

Übung 1 **Übersetze die folgenden Ausdrücke mit Präpositionen der Zeit.**

1. Am 31. Januar – ....
2. Im Sommer – ....
3. Um 5 Uhr – ....
4. Am Abend – ....
5. Am Wochenende – ....
6. In der Nacht – ....
7. Beim Frühstück – ....
8. Im Januar – ....
9. Am Dienstag – ....
10. An Weihnachten – ....

Übung 2 **Mr Johnson telefoniert mit seinem Vater. Sie besprechen, wann die Johnsons zu Besuch kommen. Setze die Präpositionen an der richtigen Stelle ein.**

during | at | on | before | in | on | until | at | at | on

Mr Johnson: Hallo Dad, how are you?

Mr Johnson senior: Oh, fine, thanks. When are you coming .... the weekend?

Mr Johnson: We want to catch the train .... Friday that leaves Canterbury .... 17.49 and arrives .... 22.06.

Mr Johnson senior: Isn't that rather late for the twins?

Mr Johnson: Yes, but .... winter the trains .... Saturdays take an hour longer.

Mr Johnson senior: Well then, it's better to travel .... Friday. Perhaps the twins can sleep .... the journey.

Mr Johnson: Yes, perhaps. But I'm sure, that when they are in bed, they will sleep .... late in the morning.

Mr Johnson senior: But let's hope that they wake up .... midday!

Lösungen Seite 114

6.2 *Prepositions of Place*/Präpositionen des Ortes

Alles klar?! **So verwendet man *Prepositions of Place*/Präpositionen des Ortes**

Präpositionen des Ortes legen ein räumliches Verhältnis fest:

Man kann mit ihnen ausdrücken, wo sich etwas befindet oder wo etwas geschieht.

in = ...

on = ...

under = ...

behind = ...

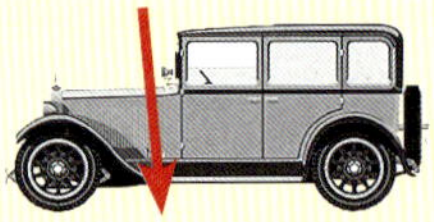

next to = ...

near = ...

in front of = ...

above = ...

between = ...

Lösungen Seite 114

Übung 1 **Übersetze die Präpositionen in den Klammern ins Englische.**

In the train to York

Mandy is sitting .... (neben) Mark in the train. They are both sitting .... (hinter) their parents. Mr Johnson put their cases above their seats .... (in) the rack (= Gepäckablage). Mark has his backpack .... (unter) his seat. There is a cup of coffee .... (auf) a small table .... (vor) Mrs Johnson and .... (zwischen) Mandy and Mark is her toy cat, which she likes to have .... (in der Nähe von) her all the time because it looks like Maggie.

Übung 2 **Beantworte die Fragen mit „Yes, she is" oder „No, she isn't."**

Where is Maggie?
Katie has stayed in Canterbury, because she doesn't want to miss her riding lesson. She is also looking after Maggie. Now it is time to feed her. But where is she? Katie looks everywhere.

Is Maggie under the table? ....

Is she on the table? ....

Is she next to the TV? ....

Is she in front of the window? ....

Is she behind the sofa? ....

Is she on the shelf above the table? ....

Is she near the door? ....

Is she between the bed and the cupboard? ....

Lösungen Seite 115

6.3 *Prepositions of Direction*/Präpositionen der Richtung

Alles klar?! **So verwendest du *Prepositions of direction***

Präpositionen der Richtung drücken aus, in welche Richtung sich etwas bewegt.

Wichtige Präpositionen, die eine Richtung ausdrücken, sind:

up = ...

down = ...

into = ...

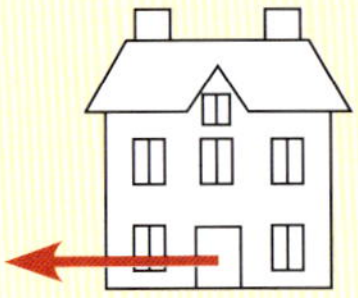
out of = ...

towards = ...

away from = ...

along = ...

(a)round = ...

through = ...

from = ...

onto = ...

over = ...

Lösungen Seite 115

Übung 1 **Übersetze die Präpositionen in Klammern.**

Jeden Morgen steigt Mr Johnson .... (auf) sein Fahrrad. Er fährt eine ruhige Straße .... (entlang), bis er die Hauptstraße erreicht. Er biegt rechts ab und fährt .... (um) das Stadttor (herum). Jetzt fährt er .... (in Richtung) des Stadtzentrums. Danach fährt er am liebsten .... (durch) den Stadtpark, aber wenn er in Eile ist, radelt er .... (über) die Hauptkreuzung, um sein Büro zu erreichen. Dort muss er nur .... (in) die Tiefgarage fahren und sein Rad abstellen.

Übung 2 **Setze die richtigen Präpositionen ein.**

Mark and Mandy want to visit the Railway Museum with Jamie and Matthew. But they do not know how to get there. Grandfather Johnson draws them a map. Can you help him with the prepositions?

over | down | behind | towards | between | over | under | up | near | along

First you walk .... the hill .... the city centre until you reach the traffic lights. Then you cross .... the road and go .... a railway bridge. After about 100 metres you turn left and walk .... a busy road. Soon you reach the river, which is very .... the museum, and then you go .... the bridge. Now you can see the museum .... some trees. The entrance (= Eingang) is .... a few steps .... two buildings.

Lerntipp

Die Verwendung von englischen Präpositionen entspricht häufig nicht der Verwendung der entsprechenden Präpositionen im Deutschen. Deshalb kann man nicht umhin, bestimmte Wendungen einfach zu lernen.

Hier bietet sich wieder die Methode mit Karteikarten und Klebezetteln an (vgl. Seite 22).

Lösungen Seite 115

Übung 3 **Finde jeweils die deutsche Bedeutung heraus.**

at

at home ....
at work ....
at school ....
at sports ....
at the front (of the class) ....
at the back (of the class) ....

in

in pencil/ink ....
in the picture ....
in German ....
in the street ....
in my opinion ....

by

by bus ....
by car ....
by mistake ....
by heart ....
by the way ....

on

on holiday ....
on the radio/TV ....
on the phone ....
on the blackboard ....
on the internet ....
on the right/left ....
on time ....

for

for breakfast ....
for lunch ....
for a week ....
for example ....

to

to England ....
from nine to five ....
20 (minutes) to five ....

Übung 4 ★ **Setze die richtigen Präpositionen ein.**

.... School

It is the Monday morning .... Mark and Mandy's trip to York, and Mark and Ben, who sit ...... the back of the class, are talking about the Railway Museum .... a geography lesson. The teacher is writing questions .... the blackboard, but Mark is drawing a picture .... pencil of the 'Flying Scotsman', one of the locomotives that he saw .... the museum. "Ben," asks the teacher, "where is the highest mountain .... Britain?" Ben doesn't hear the question, but Mark does and points .... his picture. "Scotland," Ben answers.

"And its name?", their teacher asks. "Ben Nevis, of course. I know that .... heart."

Lösungen Seite 116

STOPP!
Zuerst die Lernkärtchen durcharbeiten!

Abschlusstest (20 Minuten)

Aufgabe 1 **Setze die richtigen Präpositionen ein.**

a) Jamie, Matthew and their parents like to go walking in the Dales f.......... spring u.......... autumn.

b) Mrs Johnson gets up .... 6 o'clock to make their sandwiches b.......... breakfast.

c) They usually start out .... 8 o'clock .... the morning and finish .... about 5 o'clock .... the afternoon.

d) They stop a few times d.......... the walk to have something to drink.

e) B.......... 1 o'clock and 2 o'clock they eat their sandwiches and have a rest.

f) A.......... the walk they are very tired but happy.

Punkte: ☐ von 11

Aufgabe 2 **Übersetze die Präpositionen in Klammern.**

Mark's room is very untidy. All his books are .... (unter) his bed. His clothes are .... (auf) the chair. His football boots are .... (hinter) the cupboard. His school bag is .... (neben) his bed and his pencil case is .... (auf) the floor .... (zwischen) Mark's bed and the desk. Maggie is asleep .... (in) the middle of all this mess .... (auf) the shelf .... (über) the bed.

Punkte: ☐ von 9

Lösungen Seite 116/117

Aufgabe 3 **Setze die folgenden Präpositionen ein.**

down I above I in I into I out of I towards I up I over I in I through

Maggie sees a mouse .... the garden and runs after it .... the grass. The mouse runs .... the neighbours' garden and so Maggie jumps .... the fence. But where is the mouse now? Maggie has lost it. Then she sees a bird .... the tree .... her. She climbs .... the tree, but the bird flies away. Maggie climbs .... the tree and starts to look for the bird. Suddenly the neighbours' dog, Pluto, comes running .... her and chases her .... the garden. No luck for Maggie today!

Punkte: ☐ von 10

Aufgabe 4 **Übersetze die Präpositionen bzw. Angaben in Klammern ins Englische.**

Katie did not want to go to see her grandparents this weekend because she has riding lessons .... (am Samstag). She stayed .... (zu Hause) and .... (um) half past one she left for her lesson .... (um) two o'clock. Little Richard was .... (in) his box at the back of the stable. Katie took his saddle .... (von) the side of the box and put it .... (auf) his back. She tied the straps (= Riemen) .... (unter) his belly (= Bauch). Then she led him .... (aus) the stable and rode him .... (ins) the field for the lesson.

Punkte: ☐ von 10

Punkte: ☐ von 40

35–40: Bravo! Du weißt über die Präpositionen schon gut Bescheid.
21–34: Teilweise bist du sicher, teilweise noch nicht. Bearbeite bitte noch einmal die Übungen, in denen du beim ersten Mal viele Fehler hattest.
0–20: Leider ist dir noch zu vieles unklar. Arbeite das Kapitel bitte noch mal durch.

Lösungen Seite 117

7

Leseverstehen

The Johnsons are expecting a visit from Julia, Katie's German pen-friend, and think that she will want to know something about Canterbury. Katie has been to the library and on the internet to find out some interesting information.
She now has plenty of historical facts to tell Julia about Canterbury. This chapter will give you some ideas about how to get the most out of texts with factual information.

7.1 *Reading and Understanding*/Lesen und Verstehen

Übung 1 **Lies den Text zügig und unterstreiche die Schlüsselwörter. Einige sind bereits unterstrichen.**

Der folgende Text gibt Informationen über die Geschichte der Stadt Canterbury; es handelt sich um einen Sachtext/*factual text*. Du erfasst die Informationen am besten, wenn du die Schlüsselbegriffe/*keywords* unterstreichst und dann den Inhalt des Textes in zwei oder drei Sätzen aufschreibst.

The story of Canterbury

This is what Katie has found out about the history of Canterbury.

Thomas Beckett's murder

Canterbury, where the Johnsons live in Charlton Rd, is in the county of Kent in south-east England. Canterbury is a very old town dating from Roman times. It is not far from the coast and the port of Dover with its famous white cliffs. It is also a university town with a large student population. The town is most famous for its Cathedral, which is the centre of the Anglican Church for the whole world and the seat (= Sitz) of the Archbishop of Canterbury, who is the head of the Church in England. There is a very interesting story connected with the Cathedral: the story of Thomas Beckett, who was the adviser to the King, Henry II. In 1162 the King made Thomas the Archbishop of Canterbury. Thomas did not always agree with the King. The King was very angry because of this and four of his knights (= Ritter) went to Canterbury to do something about the situation. They murdered Thomas in the Cathedral in 1170. As a result of his death, Canterbury became a place of pilgrimage (= Pilgerfahrt) and there is a famous story by Geoffrey Chaucer called "The Canterbury Tales", written in the fourteenth century, which tells about a pilgrimage to Canterbury. In a humourous way, Chaucer describes pilgrims typical of their time such as a miller (= Müller), a cook, a lawyer (= Anwalt) and a merchant (= Kaufmann).

Tipp

Es ist nicht schlimm, wenn du ein Wort nicht kennst oder verstehst.
Man kann oft den Sinn des Textes insgesamt verstehen, ohne jedes einzelne Wort zu kennen. Bevor du in ein Wörterbuch schaust, versuche die Bedeutung selbst herauszufinden. Vielleicht kannst du sie ableiten:

- aus dem Textzusammenhang,
- wenn du ein Wort aus der gleichen Wortfamilie kennst,
- aus einem ähnlichen deutschen Wort.

Lösungen Seite 118

Übung 2 **Suche die Wörter im Text, die mit den Wörtern unten zu einer Wortfamilie gehören.**

1. law: ....
2. to sit: ....
3. to advise: ....
4. to cook: ....
5. pilgrim: ....
6. date: ....

Übung 3 **Ergänze die Sätze.**

1. Thomas Beckett was the ....
2. The Johnsons live in ....
3. Canterbury is famous for ....
4. It also has a ....
5. Dover is ....

Lösungen Seite 118

Übung 4 **Schreibe die passenden Antworten zu den Fragen aus den Kästen.**

Where is Dover?
Where do the Johnsons live?
What did Chaucer write?
Who was Thomas Beckett?
Where is Canterbury?

He was Archbishop of Canterbury.
The Canterbury Tales.
In Kent in south-east England.
On the coast.
In Canterbury.

Übung 5 **Wähle die richtige Antwort und unterstreiche sie.**

1. Geoffrey Chaucer wrote:
   a short history of Canterbury; the "Canterbury Tales"; the Life of Henry II.
2. Thomas Beckett was murdered:
   in Dover Castle; in Charlton Road; in Canterbury Cathedral.
3. Who murdered Thomas Beckett?
   Four knights; King Henry II; Mr Johnson.
4. Canterbury is situated:
   on the coast; in the south-east of England; near London.
5. Dover is famous for its:
   Harbour; coast walk; white cliffs.

Übung 6 **Schreibe die von dir unterstrichenen Wörter aus dem Text Seite 76 auf. Lies die Wörter mehrere Male laut vor.**

Übung 7 ★ **Lies den folgenden Text und beantworte die Fragen.**

Katie and the twins are spending the evening alone at home. Their parents are at the cinema. Katie likes to play games on the internet, but Mandy and Mark are too young for some of the games so they are all watching television. When the programme becomes boring (= langweilig) they play cards.

1. Where are Mr and Mrs Johnson? ....
2. What are Katie and the twins doing? ....
3. Why do they play cards? ....
4. What does Katie like to do? ....

Nun lies die Antworten laut vor.

Lösungen Seite 118/119

STOPP!
Zuerst die Lernkärtchen durcharbeiten!

Abschlusstest (20 Minuten)

Aufgabe 1 **Bringe die Satzteile in die richtige Reihenfolge.**

1. The Johnsons live/in south-east England/in Charlton Rd/in the county of Kent/ in Canterbury

   ....

2. Canterbury is/is famous for its white cliffs/not far from Dover which

   ....

3. "The Canterbury Tales" is/by Geoffrey Chaucer/a famous story

   ....

4. Chaucer describes/in his stories/typical of their time/people

   ....

5. Canterbury became/as a result of Thomas' death/a place of pilgrimage

   ....

6. The king made/the Archbishop of Canterbury/Thomas Beckett

   ....

7. Four knights murdered/on the orders of the king/Thomas Beckett

   ....

8. "The Canterbury Tales" is/written in the fourteenth century/a humorous story

   ....

Punkte: ☐ von 8

Aufgabe 2 **Setze *there is* oder *there are* in die Lücken ein.**

1. .... a famous cathedral in Canterbury.
2. .... humorous stories about pilgrims in the "Canterbury Tales".
3. .... a humorous story about Canterbury by Chaucer.
4. .... two archbishops in the Anglican Church.
5. .... an interesting story connected with the cathedral.
6. .... famous white cliffs in Dover.

Punkte: ☐ von 6

Lösungen Seite 119

Aufgabe 3 **Finde Wörter, die zur gleichen Familie wie diese Wörter im Text gehören. Nimm, wenn nötig, ein Wörterbuch zur Hand.**

fame: ....

interest: ....

anger: ....

humour: ....

advise: ....

murder: ....

agree: ....

describe: ....

Punkte: ☐ von 8

Punkte: ☐ von 22

19–22: Bravo! Dein Textverständnis ist schon sehr gut.

10–18: Teilweise bist du sicher, teilweise noch nicht. Bearbeite bitte noch einmal die Übungen, in denen du beim ersten Mal viele Fehler hattest.

0–9: Leider ist dir noch zu vieles unklar. Arbeite das Kapitel bitte noch einmal durch.

Lösungen Seite 119

8 Wortschatz und Situationen

Learning words is boring? Well, maybe. But learning words can also be fun.
On the next pages you'll find some ideas to make learning words more interesting, exciting, a game with your friends, …
When you are learning words for school next time, just have a look at the following pages and use some of the ideas – and you'll see: learning words will be a lot easier.

8.1 Den Wortschatz sichern und erweitern

Alles klar?! **Lernstrategien**

Bestimmt fragen dich deine Eltern immer wieder: Hast du denn schon deine Wörter gelernt? Manchmal hast du es sicher schon getan und bist ganz stolz auf dich. Aber manchmal sitzen die Wörter vielleicht auch noch nicht so gut.
Im Folgenden findest du einige Tipps und Tricks, was du tun kannst, um dir Wörter besser zu merken.

Lesen und Schreiben

- Wenn du einem Wort zum ersten Mal begegnest, lies es dir wiederholt laut vor und werde dabei immer leiser.
- Schließe dann die Augen und versuche, dir das Wort vorzustellen. Wenn du dir nicht sicher bist, schau dir lieber noch einmal das Schriftbild an.
- Schreibe dann das Wort auswendig auf und vergleiche es mit dem Schriftbild.

Die Echomethode

Sprich ein neues Wort erst einmal ganz laut und wiederhole es wie ein Echo immer wieder. Anschließend kannst du wieder lauter werden.

Wörter singen

Wusstest du schon, dass es dir leichter fällt, dir Wörter zu merken, wenn du sie singst? Versuche es also einmal mit Musik. Vielleicht kannst du aus mehreren Wörtern einen Rap, einen Hip-Hop, ein Lied nach deinem Lieblingsmusikstil „dichten“?

Das Hasswort

Es gibt sicher Wörter, die du dir überhaupt nicht gut merken kannst. Erkläre sie zu deinen Hasswörtern. Sprich sie ein paarmal ganz ärgerlich aus. Sage ihnen, dass du sie gar nicht magst. Du wirst sehen, plötzlich hat sich auch dieses Wort in dein Gedächtnis eingeprägt.

Der Spickzettel

Schreibe dir vor einem Vokabeltest einen „Spickzettel“. Verstecke ihn aber vor dem Test gut, damit du nicht in Gefahr kommst, ihn zu verwenden. Allein die Tastsache, dass du ihn geschrieben hast, wird dir schon helfen, dich leichter an die Wörter zu erinnern.

Alles klar?! **Wortfelder**

Wenn du ein Bild vor dir hast, kannst du dir Wörter besonders gut merken oder schon gelernte Wörter aktivieren. Beschrifte z. B. folgendes Bild mit möglichst vielen Begriffen (du musst nicht die Wörter für alle Lebensmittel kennen).

In einem zweiten Schritt kannst du dir eine Tabelle machen, in die du Wörter, die zu einem bestimmten Wortfeld gehören, einordnest.
Du kannst dir dazu deine eigenen Kategorien überlegen, z. B.:

- Food I like very much/food I don't like so much
- Food for breakfast/food for lunch/food for dinner
- Food/drink
- Fruit/vegetables/dairy products/bread and cakes

Diese Methode kannst du immer wieder bei Fotos, die du in Zeitschriften und Zeitungen findest, anwenden. So übst du deinen Wortschatz, wenn du einfach nur durch Zeitschriften blätterst.

Lösungen Seite 120

Übung 1 **Ergänze folgende Kärtchen mit Lebensmitteln deiner Wahl. Verwende dabei Wörter, die du bei der Beschriftung des Fotos gefunden hast, und Wörter, die du kennst.**

food I like very much
- ....
- ....
- ....
- ....
- ....

food I don't like so much
- ....
- ....
- ....
- ....
- ....

food for breakfast
- ....
- ....
- ....
- ....
- ....

food for lunch/dinner
- ....
- ....
- ....
- ....
- ....

drinks
- ....
- ....
- ....
- ....
- ....

fruit
- ....
- ....
- ....
- ....
- ....

dairy products
- ....
- ....
- ....
- ....
- ....

vegetables
- ....
- ....
- ....
- ....
- ....

bread and cakes
- ....
- ....
- ....
- ....
- ....

____
- ....
- ....
- ....
- ....
- ....

Lösungen Seite 120/121

Übung 2 **Hier ist ein weiteres Foto. Ergänze die Beschriftung von Körperteilen und Kleidungsstücken.**

Übung 3 **Welche Wortfelder kannst du dir anhand dieses Fotos zusammenstellen?**

- ....
- ....
- ....
- ....
- ....

- ....
- ....
- ....
- ....
- ....

- ....
- ....
- ....
- ....
- ....

- ....
- ....
- ....
- ....
- ....

Lösungen Seite 121/122

Alles klar?! **Spiele**

Die Vokabeln kannst du auch gut zusammen mit Freunden üben. Zum Beispiel könnt ihr für euch Rätsel erstellen, die ihr abwechselnd löst, oder Spiele, die ihr gemeinsam spielt.

Lückenwörter
Suche dir aus einem Wortfeld einige Begriffe aus und ersetze einzelne Buchstaben durch einen Unterstrich. Deine Freundin/dein Freund ergänzt die fehlenden Buchstaben. Dabei können z. B. die Vokale entfallen:

br_ _kf_st   s_ndw_ch

Oder, etwas schwieriger, beliebige Buchstaben:

bre_kfa_t   s_n_w_ _h

Durcheinandergewürfelte Wörter
Du kannst auch die Buchstaben ganz durcheinanderwürfeln:

abefkrast   **dinschaw**

Wörter auf den Rücken schreiben
Du kannst deiner Freundin/deinem Freund mit dem Finger Wörter auf den Rücken schreiben und sie/er rät sie.

Bilder zu Wörtern malen
Du kannst Bilder zu Wörtern malen und deine Freundin/dein Freund rät das Wort.

Lösungen Seite 122

Alles klar?! ***Word Grids*** **(Gitterrätsel)**

Du kannst *word grids* erstellen und sie deiner Freundin/deinem Freund zum Lösen geben. Am besten wählst du die Wörter aus einem bestimmten Wortfeld aus. Diese Wörter trägst du in ein Gitternetz ein und füllst anschließend die Lücken mit anderen Buchstaben.
Wenn du das *word grid* deiner Freundin/deinem Freund zum Lösen gibst, solltest du ihr/ihm sagen, wie viele Wörter du versteckt hast.
Im folgenden Word Grid sind z. B. **sechs** Wörter aus dem Wortfeld „vegetables“ versteckt, die im Plural stehen. **Kannst du sie alle finden?**

X	P	O	T	A	T	O	E	S	W	A	V	X	B
L	H	B	F	D	S	B	E	A	N	S	B	N	M
M	N	C	A	R	R	O	T	S	H	J	K	O	L
P	E	P	P	E	R	S	C	V	B	N	L	G	O
T	G	S	Q	C	U	C	U	M	B	E	R	S	U
W	O	T	O	M	A	T	O	E	S	W	M	A	B

Lösungen Seite 123

Übung 4 **Lückenwörter zum Wortfeld *vegetables*. Ergänze die fehlenden Buchstaben.**

1. p.. ..at ..	2. ..ea	3. c.. ..u.. ..er	4. b..o.. ..ol..	5. t.. ..at..
6. le.. t..ce	7. b.. ..n	8. ..ar.. ..t	9. ca..b.. ..e	10. ce..er..

Übung 5 **Lückenwörter zum Wortfeld *sports clothes*. Ergänze die fehlenden Buchstaben.**

1. sn.. ..k..rs	2. kn.. .. s..cks	3. s.. ..rts	4. j..rs.. ..	5. s..i..s..it
6. swi.. ..ing t..un..s	7. b..s..b..ll ..a..		8. f.. .t ba .. .. b.. ..ts	

Übung 6 **Bei diesen Wörtern zum Wortfeld *fruit* sind die Buchstaben etwas durcheinandergeraten. Bringe sie in die richtige Reihenfolge:**

1. alepp ....
2. aegnor ....
3. phace ....
4. aabnan ....
5. crehry ....
6. elmno ....
7. apelinepp ....
8. ragep ....
9. arep ....
10. lump ....
11. rabreprsy ....
12. wabrerrsty ....

Lösungen Seite 123

Übung 7 ★ **Hier sind die Buchstaben der Wörter zum Wortfeld *parts of the body* durcheinandergeraten. Kannst du die Buchstaben in die richtige Reihenfolge bringen?**

1. ahir ....
2. rae ....
3. edah ....
4. yee ....
5. enos ....
6. homtu ....
7. eckeh ....
8. cenk ....
9. dehlorsu ....
10. mar ....
11. dahn ....
12. fegrin ....
13. secht ....
14. achmost ....
15. gle ....
16. otof ....
17. adefehor ....
18. ceaf ....

Übung 8 **Entwickle nun dein eigenes *word grid* und gib es Freundinnen und Freunden zum Lösen.**

Lösungen Seite 123

8.2 Situationen meistern

Alles klar?! **Situations: *Asking the way***

Für bestimmte Situationen ist es gut, wenn man nicht nur die Wörter kann, sondern sich feststehende Wendungen merkt. Hier findest du sinnvolle Redemittel, wenn du dich nach dem Weg erkundigen willst bzw. nach dem Weg gefragt wirst.

Questions:

- Excuse me, where is the …, please?
- Excuse me, can you tell me the way to …, please?
- Excuse me, how do I get to …, please?
- How far is it?
- Could you show me on the map, please?

Let me repeat …

Answers:

- Turn left/right.
- Go straight ahead.
- It's the first/second/third on the left/right.
- Cross the road.
- Walk down the road.
- It's quite a long way.
- You can take the bus.
- It isn't far.
- I'm sorry, I don't know.

Other useful vocabulary:

baker's bank book shop bridge bus stop church
library market road school square street
supermarket swimming pool traffic lights …

Übung 1 **Beschreibe den Weg anhand des Plans unten.**

1. You are at the bus stop:
A: Excuse me, can you tell me the way to the station, please?

B: Yes, of course ... .

....

A: Thank you very much.

2. You are at the station:
A: Excuse me, can you tell me the way to the park, please?

B: Yes, of course ... .

....

A: Thank you very much.

3. Beschreibe einen Weg deiner Wahl.

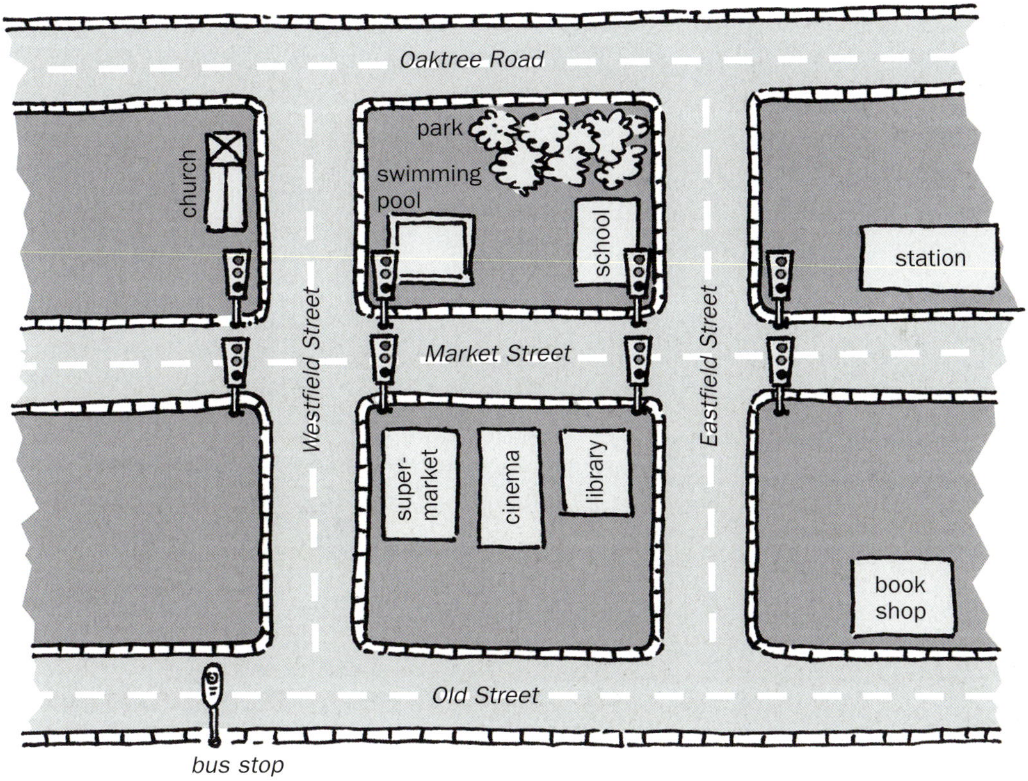

Übung 2 ★ **Zeichne die Wegbeschreibung auf.**

A: Excuse me, can you tell me the way to the swimming pool, please?
B: Yes, of course ... Go straight ahead to the end of the road and then turn left.
A: Straight ahead ... and turn left.
B Turn right at the next corner.
A: Next corner ... turn right ...
B: Go straight on and the swimming pool is 150 metres down the street on your right, opposite the school. Got it?
A: Yes I think so. Let me repeat it ... straight on ... turn left ... next corner turn right ... 150 metres on the right ... opposite school.
B: That's it.
A: Thank you very much. Goodbye.
B: Goodbye.

Lösungen Seite 124

STOPP!
Zuerst die Lernkärtchen durcharbeiten!

Abschlusstest (20 Minuten)

Aufgabe 1 **Lückenwörter zum Wortfeld *drink*. Ergänze die fehlenden Buchstaben.**

1. l .. .. on .. .. e
2. t .. ..
3. a fi .. .. y d .. .. nk
4. c .. .. f .. e
5. .. a .. er
6. c .. .. e
7. fr .. .. t j .. .. ce
8. mi .. ..

Punkte: ☐ von 8

Aufgabe 2 **Wörter mit durcheinandergeratenen Buchstaben zum Wortfeld *food for breakfast*. Bringe die Buchstaben in die richtige Reihenfolge.**

1. aledammar ....
2. bertut ....
3. egimanrar ....
4. firtu ....
5. acelres ....
6. cefefo ....
7. limk ....
8. aegnor ceiuj ....
9. ate ....
10. atsot ....

Punkte: ☐ von 10

Lösungen Seite 124

Aufgabe 3 **Beschreibe den Weg.**

You are at the book shop:

A: Excuse me, can you tell me the way to the church, please?

B: Yes, of course ... . Then .... into Westfield Street. Walk .... Westfield Street. .... Market Street. The church is .... But you can also take the bus.

A: Thank you very much.

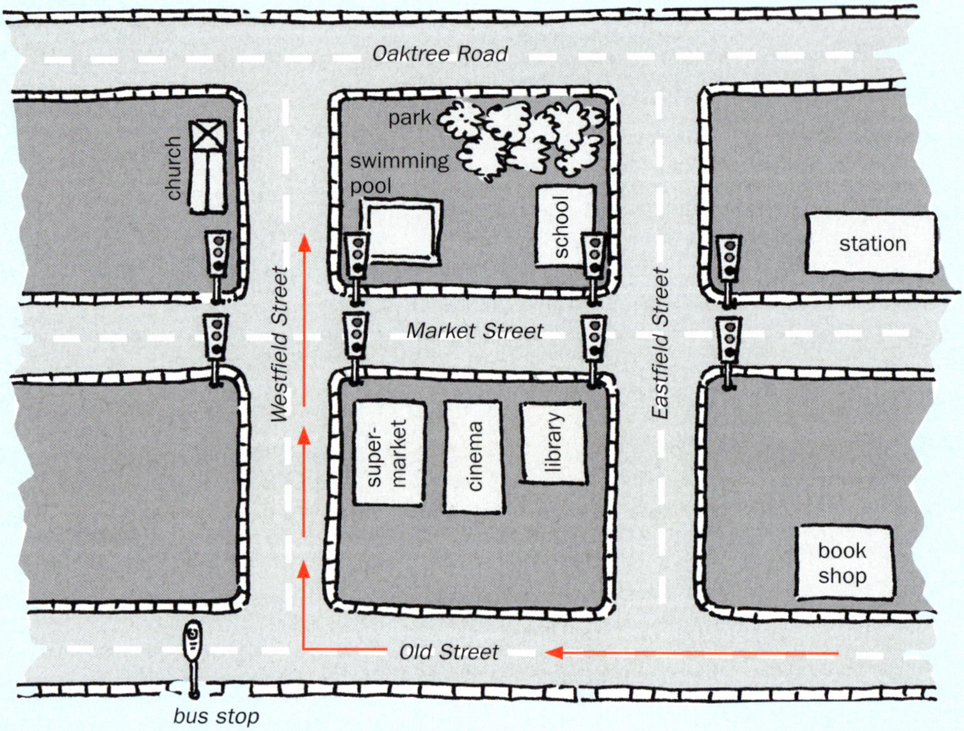

Punkte: ☐ von 5

Punkte: ☐ von 23

20–23: Bravo! Wortschatz und Wegbeschreibungen machen dir keine Schwierigkeiten.
11–19: Teilweise bist du sicher, teilweise noch nicht. Bearbeite bitte noch einmal die Übungen, in denen du beim ersten Mal viele Fehler hattest.
0–10: Leider ist dir noch zu vieles unklar. Arbeite das Kapitel bitte noch einmal durch.

Lösungen Seite 124

Lösungen

1.1 *Nouns*/Nomen

Alles klar?! (Seite 6)

cat – cats
lamp – lamps

bus – buses
house – houses

baby – babies

girl – girls
boy – boys

watch – watches
dress – dresses

hobby – hobbies

Übung 1 (Seite 6)

Singular (Einzahl)	Plural
family	families
scarf	scarves
class	classes
sandwich	sandwiches

bridge	bridges
church	churches
potato	potatoes
knife	knives
baby	babies

Übung 2 (Seite 7)

gloves	socks	shorts	glasses	trousers	scissors	shoes	pyjamas
2	1	5	6	7	3	4	8

Übung 3 (Seite 7)

1. The glasses are dirty.
2. The scissors are sharp.
3. The trousers are long.
4. The pyjamas are red.

1.2 *Articles*/Artikel

Alles klar?! (Seite 8)

- Im Englischen gibt es nur einen Artikel, im Singular wie im Plural.
- Manchmal steht im Englischen ein Artikel, im Deutschen nicht: Mark plays the recorder. – Mark spielt Blockflöte.
- Umgekehrt steht manchmal im Englischen kein Artikel, im Deutschen dagegen schon: Mahlzeiten (breakfast), Bezeichnungen von Gebäuden, wenn sie deren Funktion beschreiben (school), Straßennamen (Charlton Road), Monate (May).

Übung 1 (Seite 8)

Hi Mark,
Greetings from Wales! The weather is not very good, but the hotel is fine. It is not far from the sea and has internet access. Every morning we have breakfast before 8 o'clock and then we go by bus to visit places in the area. The people here are very friendly, but the language is difficult to understand. We often have to go into one of the shops to ask for help. In the evenings, after supper, we watch television or play cards. Hope, you are enjoying your holiday.
Love,
Ben

Übung 2 (Seite 9)

a) an umbrella
b) a banana
c) a good book
d) a young dog
e) an interesting story
f) an aeroplane
g) an old house
h) a bridge
i) an orange
j) a twin
k) an animal
l) a hobby

1.3 *Genitive*/Genitiv

Übung 1 (Seite 10)

Ben's computer
Anne's horse
Mandy's monocycle
the twins' recorders
Mr Johnson's car
the girls' pencils
Mark's inline skates
Katie's books

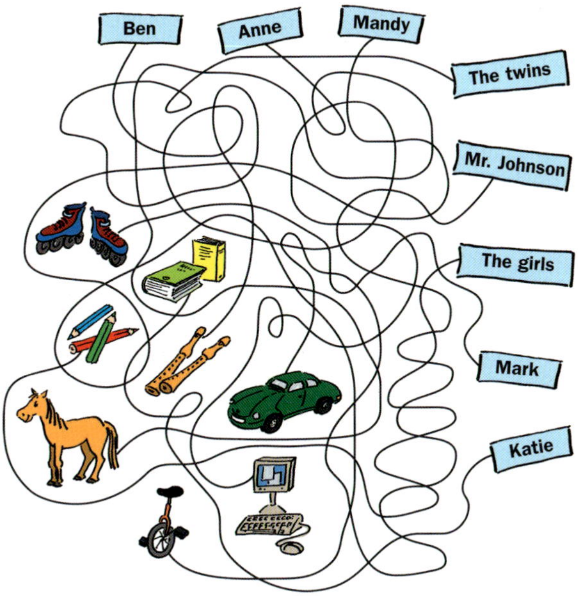

1.4 *Pronouns and Determiners*/Pronomen und Begleiter

Übung 1 (Seite 11)

1. He works in a bank.
2. They love Maggie.
3. She works in an office.
4. She is learning French.
5. It catches mice.
6. They are twins.
7. We like cooking.
8. It leaves at 12 o'clock.
9. "Will you send me an email, please?"
10. "Will you feed Maggie, please?"

Alles klar?! (Seite 12)

me – mir/mich
you – dir/dich
him – ihm/ihn
her – ihr/sie
it – ihm/es

us – uns
you – euch
them – ihnen/sie

Übung 2 (Seite 12)

1. Please, give it to Mandy.
2. Katie often plays with them.
3. These flowers are for her.
4. Can you ring him at work, please?
5. The doctor is coming to see us.
6. The teacher tells them to do their homework.
7. Please, give her the magazine.
8. Ben writes him an email.

Übung 3 (Seite 13)

Hi Julia,
My name is Katie and I am your new penfriend from England. I am thirteen years old. My father is called Phil. He is 45 years old. My mother's name is Betty, she is 40 years old. They both go out to work. I have a brother and a sister, their names are Mark and Mandy and they are twins. They are only ten years old. We live in a quiet road in a big house. It has a large garden with nice trees. We also have a cat, it is called Maggie. It is black and white and loves to play in the garden. The twins say, Maggie is their cat, I say, it is my cat. I hope, you can come for a visit soon, then you will meet my family.
Cheers,
Katie

Übung 4 (Seite 14)

1. This is the Johnson's house. This house is theirs.
2. The twins are looking for their shoes, they ask: "Are these shoes ours?"
3. This book is not Katie's book, it belongs to me, it is mine.
4. This basket is for Maggie. This basket is hers.
5. Here is a new dress for you. The dress is yours.
6. Mandy and Mark have bikes, the red one is his and the blue one is hers.

Übung 5 (Seite 15)

1.	this bike	these bikes
2.	that tree	those trees
3.	that girl	those girls
4.	this boy	these boys
5.	that house	those houses
6.	this cat	these cats
8.	that garden	those gardens
9.	this basket	these baskets
10.	that shoe	those shoes

Abschlusstest

Aufgabe 1 (Seite 16)

a) them
b) their birthday
c) its ball
d) your horse

Aufgabe 2 (Seite 16)

a) our
b) me
c) them
d) me
e) we, us
f) she

Aufgabe 3 (Seite 17)

a) Look, Mandy and Mark! They are the Johnson twins. It is their birthday and I have a present for them.
b) Mrs Johnson: "Katie, is this your French book?" Katie: "Yes, Mum, can you give it to me, please."
c) Mr Johnson is looking for his briefcase, but he can't find it.
d) "Who is that girl over there? I don't know her!"
e) "Are those children over there Mark and Mandy?" "Yes, they are playing in the garden with their cat, Maggie."
f) The twins are angry with Katie, who says Maggie is her cat. "She is not yours, she is ours," they shout.

Aufgabe 4 (Seite 17)

Ben: Hi Mark, are you going to school by bus today?
Mark: Yes, I normally go by bike, but my bike is broken. I hope to get a new mountain bike for my birthday, but mountain bikes are expensive.
Ben: I have a judo class after school today, why don't you come?
Mark: Thanks for the invitation, but I can't come. My mother is at work today and I have to feed the cat.
Ben: Can't Mandy do that? She is not at school today, is she at home?
Mark: No, she's in town. She's a girl guide and has a meeting at the church in Market Street.
Ben: What a pity! I'm sure, we will have fun and after training we all go for a hamburger.
Mark: Well, if my mother comes back from work early, maybe I can join you.
Ben: That's a good idea. See you!

Aufgabe 5 (Seite 18)

1. The Johnsons' house is in Charlton Road.
2. The twins' room has a large window.
3. The children's bikes are green and red.
4. Katie's room is very small.
5. The classrooms of the school are large.

Aufgabe 6 (Seite 18)

Mandy has
- two glasses of milk.
- three pairs of jeans.
- three pairs of pyjamas.
- one pair of scissors.

Mark says:
- "My trousers are long."
- "The glass is empty."
- "My shorts are red."
- "The glasses are dirty."

2.1 *The Simple Present*/Die einfache Gegenwart

Alles klar?! (Seite 20)

- Bei der 3. Person Singular (he/she/it) hängst du ein -s an.
- Verben, die mit einem Zischlaut [s], [z], [ʧ], [ʤ] enden: Man hängt -es an.
- Verben, die auf einen Mitlaut (Konsonant) + y enden: Das y wird zu ie, und man hängt -s an.

Übung 1 (Seite 20)

I work
He hurries
We sing
She washes
They eat

You like
He goes
I see
It starts
She fetches

Alles klar?! (Seite 21)

Singular	Plural	Singular	Plural
I am you are he is she is it is	we are you are they are	I'm you're he's she's it's	we're you're they're

Übung 2 (Seite 21)

Mandy: We must hurry, we are late for school. Where is your school bag?
Mark: It is in my room.
Mandy: Where are your shoes?
Mark: They are in the kitchen.
Mandy: Why are you so untidy?
Mark: Because I am always short of time.
Mandy: Well, that is true for both of us now!

Übung 3 (Seite 21)

Mandy: I'm really cross with Mark. We're often late for school because he never puts his things in the right place. He's the most untidy person I know. Just imagine where he puts his shoes. They're usually in the kitchen, but sometimes they're even in the bathroom.

Barbara: But you're not very tidy yourself. I'm still waiting for you to find the book you borrowed last year.

Mandy: But that's Mark's fault. It's somewhere under his bed with all the other things there.

Alles klar?! (Seite 22)

always – immer
often – oft

sometimes – manchmal
never – nie

every week – jede Woche
on Fridays – freitags

Übung 4 (Seite 23)

Katie always goes to school by bus. She likes to get to school early, so that she and her friends have time to chat, before the bell rings for the first lesson. Every week, her friend Anne tells her what fun her riding lessons are and Katie hopes that her next birthday present will be riding lessons, too. Anne says, "We often ride across the fields and sometimes we even jump over fences if they are not too high. My horse has a lovely brown coat, which I always brush after my lesson."

2.2 *The Present Progressive*/Die Verlaufsform der Gegenwart

Alles klar?! (Seite 24)

I am (I'm) reading
you are (you're) reading
he is (he's) reading
she is (she's) reading

we are (we're) reading
you are (you're) reading
they are (they're) reading

- Verben, die mit einem stummen *e* enden: Hier entfällt das e.
- Verben mit kurzem, einfachen Vokal, auf den ein Konsonant folgt: Der Konsonant wird verdoppelt.
- Verben, die auf -ie enden: Das ie wird zu einem y.

Übung 1 (Seite 24)

He is working in the garden.
She is buying food in the supermarket.
You are eating an apple.
They are waiting for the bus.

We are walking to school.
You are reading a book.
I am writing an email.
He is looking for his football boots.

Alles klar?! (Seite 25)

at the moment – im Augenblick/in diesem Moment
now – jetzt
just – gerade
Look! – Schau!

Übung 2 (Seite 25)

This afternoon Mark is playing football at school. He is running up and down the pitch. His team is leading by one goal. Their teacher calls out, "You are doing well." "I am getting thirsty," Mark thinks.
It is now half time. The boys are drinking orange juice and are having a short rest. Now the second half is beginning. The other team is trying hard to score a goal. They are passing the ball from one player to another and are waiting for a chance to shoot. Now Mark is shouting to the goalkeeper, "Look out, the ball is coming towards you!" But it's too late, it's in the net. At the moment Mark is feeling cross. "We are playing badly," he shouts out. But soon he is kicking the ball towards the goal and in it goes. His team is the winner.

2.3 *The Simple Past*/Die einfache Gegenwart

Alles klar?! (Seite 26)

- Beim *simple past* bei regelmäßigen Verben hängst du an die Grundform des Verbs -ed an.
  I played, you helped, she called
- Verben, die auf einen Konsonanten + *y* enden: Das *y* wird zu *ie*, und man hängt *-d* an.
- Verben, die mit einem stummen *-e* enden: Hier entfällt das *e*.
- Verben mit kurzem, einfachen Vokal, auf den ein Konsonant folgt: Der Konsonant wird verdoppelt.
- Unregelmäßige Bildung: *catch – caught, write – wrote, do – did*

Übung 1 (Seite 27)

They walked home.
Mr Johnson carried the bag.
The teacher opened the window.
The class learned/learnt ten new verbs.
Mark played football.
He passed the ball to the nearest player.
They planned their holiday.
Anne liked riding.

Übung 2 (Seite 27)

1. Mark ran up and down the pitch.
2. Mark's team won the match, but the other team lost.
3. They went home by bus.
4. He bought eggs for breakfast. Mark found the book and gave it to Mandy.
5. He did his homework in five minutes.
6. She saw a fox in the garden.
7. They drove to the seaside by car.
8. The school choir sang three songs.

Alles klar?! (Seite 28)

yesterday – gestern
last week – letzte Woche
two years ago – vor zwei Jahren

Übung 3 (Seite 28)

Last year Katie started secondary school in the middle of Canterbury. All week before school began, she worried about her new life, but on the first morning she woke up early and felt fine. She left home in good time for the bus, which took ten minutes to reach her school. She found everything there very exciting and soon made friends with two other pupils, Anne and Jane. She thought that the maths lesson was boring, but she liked French very much. Her teacher, Mrs James, told the class that they were all very good, but that Katie spoke French best of all.

Abschlusstest

Aufgabe 1 (Seite 29)

a) The football match is over.
b) We are the winners.
c) I am hungry.
d) Mark is untidy.
e) Mandy is cross.
f) They are late.

Aufgabe 2 (Seite 29)

a) Every morning Mandy waits for Mark.
b) He always puts his school things in the wrong place.
c) They often get to school late.
d) Katie sometimes hurries to catch the bus.
e) I like to chat with my friends every day.
f) Anne goes riding every Saturday.

Aufgabe 3 (Seite 29)

Katie is having a French lesson now. Mrs James is teaching the class new words. At present the pupils are talking to each other and some are laughing. Mrs James says to them, "Be quiet, please. You are making too much noise at the moment. I am finding it very difficult to teach you anything today."

Aufgabe 4 (Seite 30)

The twins feed Maggie every day in the morning. It is Monday morning and time to go to school. Mark is late again. He is putting Maggie's cat food into her dish now and Mandy is calling to him, "Where are you? We must go." Now they are hurrying to school and Mark is running very fast. Mandy is trying to run quickly, too. "You are going too fast," Mandy says. But now the bell is ringing for the first lesson. Mark calls out, "Hurry up, you are so slow."

Aufgabe 5 (Seite 30)

Last weekend Mandy stayed with her friend Barbara. It was Barbara's birthday and six school friends came to her party. First they played games outside. They ran round the garden playing "hide and seek". Then they ate sausages and drank lemonade. In the evening they sang songs and Mandy played her recorder. When they went to bed, they soon fell asleep.

3.1 *The Statement*/Der Aussagesatz

Alles klar?! (Seite 32)

- Bei der Verneinung wird not in Verbindung mit einem Hilfsverb gebraucht. In der gesprochenen Sprache wird hier oft die Kurzform verwendet:

  he/she/it is not ➔ he/she/it isn't *you/we/they are not ➔ you/we/they aren't*

Übung 1 (Seite 33)

1. The twins didn't visit the Tower of London.
2. Katie doesn't like travelling by train.
3. The Booths don't live in Wimbledon.
4. Ben didn't promise to take Mark to judo class.
5. Their grandparents didn't take the twins to a tennis match.
6. Anne didn't tell Katie about her riding lessons.

Alles klar?! (Seite 34)

Manche Verben können zwei Objekte haben:

- ein Dativ- oder indirektes Objekt – Frage: **Wem**?
- ein Akkusativ oder direktes Objekt – Frage: **Wen oder was**?

The twins wrote Grandma Mary a postcard.
Wem? Wen oder was?

Das indirekte Objekt steht vor dem direkten Objekt.

to bring	bringen	to read	lesen
to buy	kaufen	to send	schicken
to give	geben	to show	zeigen
to make	machen	to take	nehmen
to pay	bezahlen	to tell	erzählen
to promise	versprechen	to write	schreiben

Übung 2 (Seite 34)

1. The sports teacher throws the ball to Ben.
2. Mr Johnson washes the car every Saturday.
3. The twins play the recorder in the orchestra.
4. Mark and Mandy give the cat its food every morning.
5. Katie brushes the horse after the riding lesson.
6. Ben eats an apple for lunch at school.
7. Mark scores a goal in the football game.
8. Katie reads a book in the evening.

Übung 3 (Seite 35)

1. The twins gave the cat its food.
2. Johnson promised the children a trip to London.
3. Mrs Johnson wrote her mother a letter.
4. Katie showed Anne the email.
5. Mrs Johnson bought the twins an ice cream.
6. The twins sent their friend a postcard.
7. Grandma Mary made the twins a cake.
8. The teacher told the class a story.

Übung 4 (Seite 35)

1. The policeman showed the children the way to the Tower.
2. Anne wrote her friend a letter.
3. Mr and Mrs Johnson bought Mark a new mountain bike.
4. Ben sent Mandy an email.
5. Mother makes Katie a birthday cake every year.
6. Grandma tells the twins a story every evening.
7. The teacher took his class to the museum.
8. My mother promised me a red dress for Christmas.

3.2 *Questions*/Fragen

Übung 1 (Seite 36/37)

1. Does Mrs Johnson work for the church?
2. Did they go to London by car?
3. Are the twins watching the Changing of the Guard?
4. Did they visit Buckingham Palace last year?
5. Does Maggie like to catch mice?
6. Do the twins like playing the recorder?

Übung 2 (Seite 37)

1. Does Anne like riding? Yes, she does.
2. Did Mark go to judo? No, he didn't.
3. Are the guards at the Tower called Beefeaters? Yes, they are.
4. Did the Johnsons go to London by car? Yes, they did.
5. Do the twins have inline skates? No, they don't.
6. Does Ben have a horse? No, he doesn't.

Alles klar?! (Seite 38)

Fragen mit Fragewörtern

who?	wer?	*which?*	welche/r/s?
where?	wo?	*when?*	wann?
why?	warum?	*what?*	was?
how?	wie?	*whose?*	wessen?

who likes picnics?

S P O

Übung 3 (Seite 39)

1. Where do the Johnsons live?
2. When does the train leave?
3. How many windows does the house have?
4. Who is riding Anne's horse?
5. What do the twins have for their picnic?
6. How much milk is left in the glass?
7. Why did Katie stay at home?
8. When does the church bell ring?
9. Where is Maggie sleeping?
10. Who lives in Wimbledon?

3.3 *Imperatives*/Befehlsform

Übung 1 (Seite 40)

1. You are late for school, Mark. Hurry up.
2. We are tired. Let us (Let's) go home.
3. (Mark to his father) I kicked the ball through the window. Don't be angry.
4. (Mr Johnson to Mark) Next time be more careful.

3.4 *Subordinate Clauses*/Nebensätze

Alles klar?! (Seite 41)

Auch in Nebensätzen gilt die Wortstellung **S – P – O**.

before	vor
but	aber
when	wenn, als

Übung 1 (Seite 41)

1. … because the weather is fine.
2. Before the Johnsons take the Underground …
3. When they reach the boat …
4. … because they do not (don't) go on the trip.

Abschlusstest

Aufgabe 1 (Seite 42)

a) Katie isn't doing her French homework in her room.
b) The Booths live in Wimbledon.
c) Mandy didn't send Anne an email.
d) The twins haven't got a television in their room.
e) Anne brushes her horse every day.
f) The Johnsons had a picnic in the park.

Aufgabe 2 (Seite 42/43)

a) Do you come from Canterbury?
b) Do your parents live in London?
c) Does your friend live in Charlton Rd?
d) Did you and Ben meet in London?
e) Do you like judo?
f) Do you like all subjects at school?

Aufgabe 3 (Seite 43)

a) Who has a riding lesson every Saturday?
b) What is Katie reading?
c) Where do the twins play football?
d) What does Mr Johnson own?
e) Where did we go last week?
f) When is Ben's birthday?
g) Where is the Johnson's house?
h) Why do the twins like inline skating?
i) Who guards the Tower of London?
j) Why are we going to school by bus today?

Aufgabe 4 (Seite 44)

a) Katie's mother wrote the teacher a letter.
b) Mother promised me a new dress for Christmas.
c) The teacher took the children to the museum.
d) The policeman showed them the way to the Tower.

Aufgabe 5 (Seite 44)

a) When you visit the Tower of London, look out for the ravens.
b) Their wings are clipped because they must stay in the Tower.
c) When you see the Crown Juwels, don't miss the Koh-i-Noor diamond.
d) It is famous because it is one of the largest diamonds in the world.

4.1 *Numbers/Zahlen*

Alles klar?! (Seite 46)

Mit Cardinal Numbers/Grundzahlen warden Dinge oder Lebewesen gezählt.

1 = one	6 = six	11 = eleven	16 = sixteen
2 = two	7 = seven	12 = twelve	17 = seventeen
3 = three	8 = eight	13 = thirteen	18 = eighteen
4 = four	9 = nine	14 = fourteen	19 = nineteen
5 = five	10 = ten	15 = fifteen	20 = twenty

Zehnerzahl steht vor Einerzahl, verbunden mit Bindestrich.
twenty-one – twenty-two – twenty-three – twenty-four

Übung 1 (Seite 47)

Today is March 15th. It is Katie's birthday. She is fourteen. Look at all her presents. She has four books, three CDs, two pairs of trousers and eighteen birthday cards. In one of them is a voucher (= Gutschein) for ten riding lessons. She is very happy now. At her party Mark and Mandy play six of Katie's favourite tunes (= Lieblingsmelodien) on their recorders. They also give her three pictures of Maggie, which they painted themselves. And what did Maggie give her? One dead mouse, of course.

Übung 2 (Seite 48)

1. How many months does a year have? 12
2. How many days does a week have? 7
3. How many hours are there in a day? 24
4. How many minutes are there in an hour? 60
5. How many days does March have? 31
6. How many legs does an insect have? 6
7. How many rings does the Olympic flag have? 5
8. How many days are there in a year? 365 or 366

Übung 3 (Seite 48)

1. eight – five – nine – six – 0 – seven – one
2. seven – nine – three – four – five – one – two
3. four – eight – four – eight – six – two – five
4. one – 0 – nine – six – seven – four – five

Übung 4 (Seite 49)

computer

1. Christmas
2. London
3. Wimbledon
4. Paris
5. Judo Club
6. Canterbury
7. Berlin
8. Germany

4.2 *Time*/Uhrzeit

Alles klar?! (Seite 50)

- Für Uhrzeiten zwischen der vollen und der halben Stunde verwendet man ***past*** (nach), ab der 31. Minute ***to*** (vor).
- Vor dem Mittag wird in der Regel mit Zusatz **am** versehen, nach dem Mittag **pm**.

in the morning	am Morgen
in the afternoon	am Nachmittag
in the evening	am Abend
at night	in der Nacht

Übung 1 (Seite 51)

a) three o'clock
b) a quarter past six
c) five past ten
d) twenty-five to nine
e) half past two
f) a quarter to ten
g) ten to six
h) twenty past twelve

Übung 2 (Seite 51)

a) wrist watch b) pocket watch c) alarm clock d) church clock e) grandfather clock

Übung 3 (Seite 52)

1. When does school start? At nine o'clock.
2. When does Mandy and Mark's lunch break start? At half past twelve.
3. When does school begin in the afternoon? At two o'clock.
4. When does football practice start? At half past four.
5. When does Mandy go home on Monday and Thursday? At four o'clock.
6. When does orchestra practice begin? At half past four.
7. When do Mandy and Mark go home on Wednesday? At six o'clock.
8. When do Mandy and Mark go to the Judo club? At six o'clock.

4.3 *Dates*/Datumsangaben

Alles klar?! (Seite 53)

Verkürzte Schreibweise:

08/05/2008	8. Mai 2008 (GB)
	5. August 2008 (USA)

Übung 1 (Seite 54)

1. 29th December/December 29th 2007
2. 7th August/August 7th 2001
3. 11th November/November 11th 1996
4. 3rd June/June 3rd 1999
5. 12th January/January 12th 2000
6. 15th July/July 15th 1982
7. 22nd October/October 22nd 2002
8. 9th April/April 9th 2003

Übung 2 (Seite 54)

1. March the fifth
2. August the second
3. the twenty-seventh of February
4. June the sixteenth
5. November the fourth
6. the twenty-fifth of September
7. January the third
8. the first of December

Abschlusstest

Aufgabe 1 (Seite 55)

a) 22: twenty-two
b) 15: fifteen
c) 74: seventy-four
d) 42: forty-two
e) 55: fifty-five
f) 96: ninety-six
g) 111: a hundred and eleven
h) 89: eighty-nine
i) 12: twelve
j) 247: two hundred and forty-seven

Aufgabe 2 (Seite 55)

Little Richard

Aufgabe 3 (Seite 55)

1. (18.30) It's half past six in the evening.
2. (13.20) It's twenty past one in the afternoon.
3. (9.45) It's a quarter to ten in the morning.
4. (4.55) It's five to five in the morning.
5. (16.25) It's twenty-five past four in the afternoon.
6. (19.00) It's seven o'clock in the evening.
7. (1.05) It's five past one at night.
8. (6.50) It's ten to seven in the morning.

Aufgabe 4 (Seite 56)

1. On which day of the week do Mandy and Mark have orchestra practice?
   On Wednesday.
2. On which days of the week does Mark have football practice?
   On Monday and Thursday.
3. On which day of the week do Mark and Mandy go to the Judo club?
   On Friday.
4. On which day of the week do both twins go home at 4 o'clock?
   On Tuesday.

Aufgabe 5 (Seite 56)

Hi Katie,
You wanted to know, when our birthdays are. My father's birthday is on 10th October/October 10th. My mother's birthday is on 4th January. My brother's birthday is on March 7th/7th March. My birthday is on August 15th, when I hope to get lots of presents.
Hope to hear from you soon,
Julia

5.1 *Adverbial Phrases of Place*/Ortsangaben

Übung 1 (Seite 58)

1. Katie's grandparents live in Wimbledon.
2. The twins play football in the garden.
3. Mrs Johnson works in the church office.
4. Maggie sleeps in her basket.

5.2 *Adverbial Phrases of Time*/Zeitangaben

Übung 1 (Seite 59)

1. The twins go to primary school in Canterbury every day / Every day the twins go to primary school in Canterbury.
2. British pupils start secondary school when they are eleven.
3. Katie must wear a school uniform at her school.
4. The twins can have lunch at school.
5. Katie has her music lesson at school.
6. Every Saturday Ann has her riding lesson at the riding school / Ann has her riding lesson at the riding school every Saturday.

Übung 2 (Seite 60)

1. Mr Johnson goes to the office early in the morning.
2. The family is going on a trip to Dover today.
3. The journey to Dover takes one hour.
4. The visit to Dover Castle is in the afternoon.
5. On Sundays the Johnsons visit their grand-parents.
6. The twins play the recorder in the school orchestra on Tuesdays.

Übung 3 (Seite 61)

1. The twins go to junior school in Canterbury.
2. Katie wants to visit her friend in Broadstairs at the weekend.
3. Mark sees Ben at the bus stop every morning.
4. The twins have a recorder lesson at school every day.
5. Katie goes to her riding lesson after school.
6. The Johnsons are visiting the castle in Dover on Saturday.

5.3 *Adverbial Phrases of Frequency*/Häufigkeitsangaben

Alles klar?! (Seite 62)

Häufigkeitsangaben stehen zwischen dem Subjekt und dem Prädikat eines Satzes.
never – sometimes – often – usually – always

Übung 1 (Seite 62)

sometimes never usually
always often

Übung 2 (Seite 62)

1. Katie sometimes forgets her French homework.
2. The Johnsons often visit Mrs Johnson's parents in London.
3. The twins never go to school by bus.
4. Mrs Johnson usually works in the church office.
5. Ben and Mark sometimes go to the judo club on Tuesday.
6. Maggie always sleeps in her basket.

Abschlusstest

Aufgabe 1 (Seite 62)

a) manchmal – sometimes
b) nie – never
c) immer – always
d) gewöhnlich – usually
e) häufig – often

Aufgabe 2 (Seite 63)

a) We usually go to school by bike.
b) The Johnsons often spend the weekend in Broadstairs.
c) Katie and the twins sometimes visit their grandparents together.
d) Mrs Johnson always does the shopping at the supermarket.
e) Anne never forgets to brush her horse after riding.
f) Mr Johnson usually leaves the office at 5 pm.

Aufgabe 3 (Seite 64)

a). The school bus usually leaves the bus stop at 8 o'clock.
b) Katie and Anne always go riding at 10 am on Saturdays.
c) In summer the children often go swimming in the open-air pool at the beach.
d) Katie never does her homework at the table in the dining-room.
e) In summer the French teacher sometimes travels to Paris in France.
f) Mr and Mrs Johnson often go to the cinema at the weekend.

6.1 *Prepositions of Time*/Präpositionen der Zeit

Alles klar?! (Seite 66)

- Mit Präpositionen der Zeit kannst ausdrücken, wann oder wie lange etwas geschieht.
- Längere Zeitabschnitte: **in**
- Wochentage oder Datumsangaben: **on**
- Bestimmter Zeitpunkt: **at**

before = vor
after = nach
during = während
until = bis
between = zwischen
from … until/to = von … bis

Übung 1 (Seite 67)

1. Am 31. Januar – on 31st January/on January 31st
2. Im Sommer – in summer
3. Um 5 Uhr – at 5 o'clock
4. Am Abend – in the evening
5. Am Wochenende – at the weekend
6. In der Nacht – at night
7. Beim Frühstück – at breakfast
8. Im Januar – in January
9. Am Dienstag – on Tuesday
10. An Weihnachten – at Christmas

Übung 2 (Seite 67)

Mr Johnson:	Hello Dad, how are you?
Mr Johnson senior:	Oh, fine thanks. When are you coming at the weekend?
Mr Johnson:	We want to catch the train on Friday that leaves Canterbury at 17.49 and arrives at 22.06.
Mr Johnson senior:	Isn't that rather late for the twins?
Mr Johnson:	Yes, but in winter the trains on Saturdays take an hour longer.
Mr Johnson senior:	Well then, it's better to travel on Friday. Perhaps the twins can sleep during the journey.
Mr Johnson:	Yes, perhaps. But I'm sure, that when they are in bed, they will sleep until late in the morning.
Mr Johnson senior:	But let's hope, that they wake up before midday!

6.2 *Prepositions of Place*/Präpositionen des Ortes

Alles klar?! (Seite 68)

Präpositionen des Ortes legen ein räumliches Verhältnis fest: Wo befindet sich etwas oder wo geschieht etwas?

in = in
under = unter
next to = neben
in front of = vor
between = zwischen
on = auf
behind = hinter
near = in der Nähe von
above = oberhalb, über

Übung 1 (Seite 69)

Mandy is sitting next to Mark in the train. They are both sitting behind their parents. Mr Johnson put their cases above their seats in the rack (= Gepäckablage). Mark has his backpack under his seat. There is a cup of coffee on a small table in front of Mrs Johnson and between Mandy and Mark is her toy cat, which she likes to have near her all the time because it looks like Maggie.

Übung 2 (Seite 69)

Is Maggie under the table? No, she isn't.
Is she on the table? No, she isn't.
Is she next to the TV? No, she isn't.
Is she in front of the window? No, she isn't.
Is she behind the sofa? No, she isn't.
Is she on the shelf above the table? No, she isn't.
Is she near the door? No, she isn't.
Is she between the bed and the cupboard? Yes, she is.

6.3 *Prepositions of Direction*/Präpositionen der Richtung

Alles klar?! (Seite 70)

Präpositionen der Richtung drücken aus, in welche Richtung sich etwas bewegt.

up = nach oben, hinauf
down = nach unten, hinunter
into = in … hinein
out of = aus … heraus
towards = auf … zu
away from = weg von
along = entlang
(a)round = um … herum
through = durch
from = aus, von
onto = auf
over = über

Übung 1 (Seite 71)

on (auf)
along (entlang)
round (um … herum)
towards (in Richtung)
through (durch)
over (über)
into (in)

Übung 2 (Seite 71)

First you walk down the hill towards the city centre until you reach the traffic lights. Then you cross over the road and go under a railway bridge. After about 100 metres you turn left and walk along a busy road. Soon you reach the river, which is very near the museum, and then you go over the bridge. Now you can see the museum behind some trees. The entrance (= Eingang) is up a few steps between two buildings.

Übung 3 (Seite 72)

at at home = zu Hause at work = bei der Arbeit at school = in der Schule at sports = beim Sport at the front (of the class) = vorne (im Klassen-zimmer) at the back (of the class) = hinten (im Klas-senzimmer)	**in** in pencil/ink = mit Bleistift/Tinte in the picture = auf dem Bild in German = auf Deutsch in the street = auf der Straße in my opinion = meiner Meinung nach
by by bus = mit dem Bus by car = mit dem Auto by mistake = aus Versehen by heart = auswendig by the way = übrigens	**on** on holiday = im Urlaub on the radio/TV = im Radio/Fernsehen on the phone = am Telefon on the blackboard = an der Tafel on the internet = im Internet on the right/left = rechts/links on time = pünktlich
for for breakfast = zum Frühstück for lunch = zum Mittagessen for a week = eine Woche lang for example = zum Beispiel	**to** to England = nach England from nine to five = von neun bis fünf Uhr 20 (minutes) to five = 20 (Minuten) vor fünf

Übung 4 (Seite 72)

At School
It is the Monday morning after Mark and Mandy's trip to York, and Mark and Ben, who sit at the back of the class, are talking about the Railway Museum during a geography lesson. The teacher is writing questions on the blackboard, but Mark is drawing a picture in pencil of the 'Flying Scotsman', one of the locomotives, that he saw in the museum. "Ben," asks the teacher, "where is the highest mountain in Britain?" Ben doesn't hear the question, but Mark does and points to his picture. "Scotland," Ben answers.
"And its name?", their teacher asks. "Ben Nevis, of course. I know that by heart."

Abschlusstest

Aufgabe 1 (Seite 73)

a) Jamie, Matthew and their parents like to go walking in the Dales from spring until autumn.
b) Mrs Johnson gets up at 6 o'clock to make their sandwiches before breakfast.
c) They usually start out at 8 o'clock in the morning and finish at about 5 o'clock in the afternoon.
d) They stop a few times during the walk to have something to drink.
e) Between 1 o'clock and 2 o'clock they eat their sandwiches and have a rest.
f) After the walk they are very tired but happy.

Aufgabe 2 (Seite 73)

Mark's room is very untidy. All his books are under his bed. His clothes are on the chair. His football boots are behind the cupboard. His school bag is next to his bed and his pencil case is on the floor between Mark's bed and the desk. Maggie is asleep in the middle of all this mess on the shelf above the bed.

Aufgabe 3 (Seite 74)

Maggie sees a mouse in the garden and runs after it through the grass. The mouse runs into the neighbours' garden and so Maggie jumps over the fence. But where is the mouse now? Maggie has lost it. Then she sees a bird in the tree above her. She climbs up the tree, but the bird flies away. Maggie climbs down the tree and starts to look for the bird. Suddenly the neighbours' dog, Pluto, comes running towards her and chases her out of the garden. No luck for Maggie today!

Aufgabe 4 (Seite 74)

Katie did not want to go to see her grandparents this weekend because she has riding lessons on Saturdays. She stayed at home and at half past one she left for her lesson at two o'clock. Little Richard was in his box at the back of the stable. Katie took his saddle from the side of the box and put it on/onto his back. She tied the straps (= Riemen) under his belly (= Bauch). Then she led him out of the field for the lesson.

7.1 *Reading and Understanding*/Lesen unsd Verstehen

Übung 1 (Seite 76)

Canterbury, where the Johnsons live in Charlton Rd, is in the county of Kent in south-east England. Canterbury is a very old town dating from Roman times. It is not far from the coast and the port of Dover with its famous white cliffs. It is also a university town with a large student population. The town is most famous for its Cathedral, which is the centre of the Anglican Church for the whole world and the seat (= Sitz) of the Archbishop of Canterbury, who is the head of the Church in England. There is a very interesting story connected with the Cathedral: the story of Thomas Beckett, who was the adviser to the King, Henry II. In 1162 the King made Thomas the Archbishop of Canterbury. Thomas did not always agree with the King. The King was very angry because of this and four of his knights (= Ritter) went to Canterbury to do something about the situation. They murdered Thomas in the Cathedral in 1170. As a result of his death, Canterbury became a place of pilgrimage (= Pilgerfahrt) and there is a famous story by Geoffrey Chaucer called "*The Canterbury Tales*", written in the fourteenth century, which tells about a pilgrimage to Canterbury. In a humourous way, Chaucer describes pilgrims typical of their time such as a miller (= Müller), a cook, a lawyer (= Anwalt) and a merchant (= Kaufmann).

Die kurze Inhaltsangabe könnte so aussehen:
Canterbury, which is a very old town in Kent in south east England, is near Dover and the coast. It has a university and a cathedral, and its Archbishop is also the head of the Church of England. After the murder of Archbishop Thomas Beckett in the Cathedral in 1170, Canterbury became a place of pilgrimage, which Chaucer famously wrote about in his "Canterbury Tales".

Übung 2 (Seite 77)

1. law: lawyer
2. to sit: seat
3. to advise: adviser
4. to cook: cook
5. pilgrim: pilgrimage
6. date: dating

Übung 3 (Seite 77)

1. Thomas Beckett was the Archbishop of Canterbury.
2. The Johnsons live in Charlton Road.
3. Canterbury is famous for its Cathedral.
4. It also has a university.
5. Dover is famous for its white cliffs.

Übung 4 (Seite 78)

Where is Dover? On the coast.
Where do the Johnsons live? In Canterbury.
What did Chaucer write? The Canterbury Tales.
Who was Thomas Beckett? He was Archbishop of Canterbury.
Where is Canterbury? In Kent in south-east England.

Übung 5 (Seite 78)

1. Geoffrey Chaucer wrote: the "Canterbury Tales".
2. Thomas Beckett was murdered: in Canterbury Cathedral.
3. Who murdered Thomas Beckett: four knights.
4. Canterbury is situated: in the south-east of England.
5. Dover is famous for its: white cliffs.

Übung 7 (Seite 78)

1. Where are Mr and Mrs Johnson? They are at the cinema.
2. What are Katie and the twins doing? They are watching television.
3. Why do they play cards? They play cards because the TV programme is boring.
4. What does Katie like to do? Katie likes to play games on the internet.

Abschlusstest

Aufgabe 1 (Seite 79)

1. The Johnsons live in Charlton Rd in Canterbury in the country of Kent in south-east England.
2. Canterbury is not far from Dover, which is famous for its white cliffs.
3. "The Canterbury Tales" is a famous story by Geoffrey Chaucer.
4. Chaucer describes people typical of their time in his stories.
5. Canterbury became a place of pilgrimage as a result of Thomas' death.
6. The king made Thomas Beckett the Archbishop of Canterbury.
7. Four knights murdered Thomas Beckett on the orders of the king.
8. "The Canterbury Tales" is a humorous story written in the fourteenth century.

Aufgabe 2 (Seite 79)

1. There is a famous cathedral in Canterbury.
2. There are humorous stories about pilgrims in the "Canterbury Tales".
3. There is a humorous story about Canterbury by Chaucer.
4. There are two archbishops in the Anglican Church.
5. There is an interesting story connected with the cathedral.
6. There are famous white cliffs in Dover.

Aufgabe 3 (Seite 80)

fame: famous
interest: interesting
anger: angry
humour: humorous
advise: adviser
murder: murderer
agree: agreement
describe: description

8.1 Wortschatz sichern und erweitern

Alles klar?! (Seite 83)

Übung 1 (Seite 84)

Beispiellösung:

food I like very much	**food I don't like so much**
• pasta • cheese • chocolate • fruit • croissant …	• cabbage • leek • margarine • beans …
food for breakfast • marmalade • butter • margarine • fruit • cereals (cornflakes, cheerios, …) • coffee • milk • orange juice • tea • toast …	**food for lunch/dinner** • pasta • potatoes • roast • sandwich • snacks • soup • vegetables …

drinks • a fizzy drink • coffee • coke • fruit juice • lemonade • milk • tea • water …	**fruit** • apple • banana • cherry • lemon • orange • peach • pineapple • plum • strawberry …
dairy products • butter • cheese • cream • ice cream • milk • yoghurt …	**vegetables** • beans • broccoli • cabbage • carrot • cucumber • peas • potato • tomato …
bread and cakes • bagel • biscuit • bread • cake • croissant • roll • toast …	• …

Übung 2 (Seite 85)

Übung 3 (Seite 85)

Lösungsvorschlag

parts of the body	**sports clothes**
• arm • cheek • chest • ear • eye • face • finger • foot • forehead • hair • hand • head • leg • mouth • neck • nose • shoulder • stomach • …	• (knee) socks • (swimming) trunks • baseball cap • football boots • jersey • shorts • sneakers • swimsuit • …
sports • basketball • football • handball • tennis • …	**other clothes** • jacket • jeans • shoe • trousers • T-shirt • …

Alles klar?! (Seite 86)

Lückenwörter

breakfast sandwich
breakfast sandwich

Durcheinandergewürfelte Wörter

abefkrast: breakfast
dinschaw: sandwich

Alles klar?! (Seite 87)

Gitterrätsel

X	P	O	T	A	T	O	E	S	W	A	V	X	B
L	H	B	F	D	S	B	E	A	N	S	B	N	M
M	N	C	A	R	R	O	T	S	H	J	K	O	L
P	E	P	P	E	R	S	C	V	B	N	L	G	O
T	G	S	Q	C	U	C	U	M	B	E	R	S	U
W	O	T	O	M	A	T	O	E	S	W	M	A	B

Übung 4 (Seite 88)

1. potato
2. pea
3. cucumber
4. broccoli
5. tomato
6. lettuce
7. bean
8. carrot
9. cabbage
10. celery

Übung 5 (Seite 88)

1. sneakers
2. knee socks
3. shorts
4. jersey
5. swimsuit
6. swimming trunks
7. baseball cap
8. football boots

Übung 6 (Seite 88)

1. apple
2. orange
3. peach
4. banana
5. cherry
6. lemon
7. pineapple
8. grape
9. pear
10. plum
11. raspberry
12. strawberry

Übung 7 (Seite 89)

1. hair
2. ear
3. head
4. eye
5. nose
6. mouth
7. cheek
8. neck
9. shoulder
10. arm
11. hand
12. finger
13. chest
14. stomach
15. leg
16. foot
17. forehead
18. face

8.2 Situationen meistern

Übung 1 (Seite 91)

1. A: Excuse me, can you tell me the way to the station, please?
   B: Yes, of course … Go straight ahead until you reach the next corner. Turn left into Eastfield Street, at the traffic lights turn right into Market Street. The station is on your left. But you can also take the bus.
   A: Thank you very much.
2. A: Excuse me, can you tell me the way to the park, please?
   B: Yes, of course … Walk down Market Street. Turn right into Eastfield Street and cross the road. Go straight ahead. At the next corner turn left into Oaktree Road. The Park is right there.
   A: Thank you very much.

Übung 2 (Seite 92)

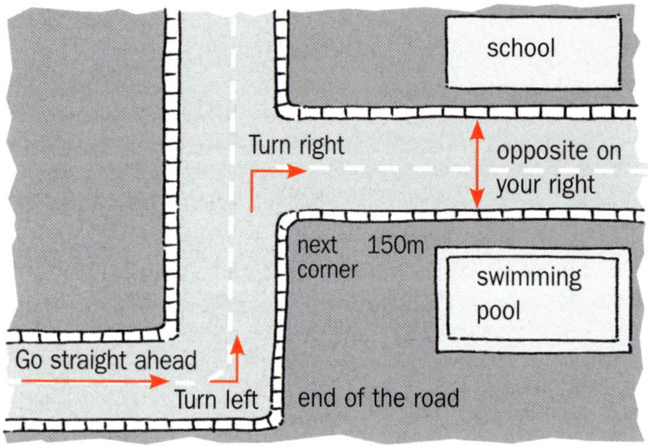

Abschlusstest

Aufgabe 1 (Seite 93)

1. lemonade
2. tea
3. a fizzy drink
4. coffee
5. water
6. coke
7. fruit juice
8. milk

Aufgabe 2 (Seite 93)

1. marmalade
2. butter
3. margarine
4. fruit
5. cereals
6. coffee
7. milk
8. orange juice
9. tea
10. toast

Aufgabe 3 (Seite 94)

A: Excuse me, can you tell me the way to the church, please?
B: Yes, of course … Go straight ahead. Then turn right into Westfield Street. Walk along Westfield Street. Cross Market Street. The church is on your left. But you can also take the bus.
A: Thank you very much.

Wichtige unregelmäßige Verben

Infinitiv	Past Simple	Deutsch
be	was/were	sein
begin	began	beginnen, anfangen
break	broke	brechen
bring	brought	bringen
build	built	bauen
buy	bought	kaufen
catch	caught	fangen
choose	chose	wählen
come	came	kommen
cost	cost	kosten
cut	cut	schneiden
do	did	tun, machen
draw	drew	zeichnen
drink	drank	trinken
drive	drove	fahren
eat	ate	essen
fall	fell	fallen
feed	fed	füttern
feel	felt	fühlen
fight	fought	kämpfen
find	found	finden
forget	forgot	vergessen
get	got	bekommen
give	gave	geben
go	went	gehen
grow	grew	wachsen
have	had	haben
hear	heard	hören
hide	hid	verstecken
hit	hit	schlagen, treffen
hold	held	halten
hurt	hurt	verletzen
keep	kept	behalten
know	knew	kennen, wissen
lay	laid	legen

Infinitiv	Past Simple	Deutsch
lead	led	führen, leiten
leave	left	verlassen
let	let	lassen
lie	lay	liegen
lose	lost	verlieren
make	made	machen
mean	meant	bedeuten
meet	met	treffen
pay	paid	bezahlen
put	put	setzen, stellen, legen
read	read	lesen
ride	rode	reiten
ring	rang	klingeln
rise	rose	aufgehen
run	ran	rennen
say	said	sagen
see	saw	sehen
sell	sold	verkaufen
send	sent	schicken
set	set	setzen, stellen
sing	sang	singen
sit	sat	sitzen
sleep	slept	schlafen
speak	spoke	sprechen
spend	spent	ausgeben, verbringen
stand	stood	stehen
steal	stole	stehlen
swim	swam	schwimmen
take	took	nehmen, dauern
teach	taught	unterrichten
tell	told	erzählen
think	thought	denken
throw	threw	werfen
understand	understood	verstehen
wear	wore	tragen (Kleidung)
write	wrote	schreiben

Stichwortfinder

Adverbial Phrases 58, 59, 62
Article 8, 9
Artikel 8, 9
Asking the way 90
Aussagesatz 32

Befehlsform 40

Cardinal Numbers 46

Dates 53
Datumsangaben 53
Demonstrative Pronouns 15
Demonstrativpronomen 15

Echomethode 82

Fragen 36–39
Fragen mit Fragewort 38

Gegenwart, einfache 20
Gegenwart, Verlaufsform 24
Genitiv 10
Genitive 10
Grundzahlen 46

Hasswort 82
Häufigkeitsangaben 62
How many und *How much* 39

Imperatives 40

Ja-/Nein-Fragen 36

Kurzantworten 37

Lernstrategien 82
Lesen und Schreiben 82
Lesen und Verstehen 76
Lückenwörter 86

Nebensätze 41
Nomen 6, 7
Nouns 6, 7

of-Genitive 10
Ordinal Numbers 49
Ordnungszahlen 49
Ortsangaben 58

Paarwörter 7
Pair words 7
Personalpronomen 11, 12
Personal Pronouns 11, 12
Possessivbegleiter
und -pronomen 13, 14
Possessive Determiners
and Pronouns 13, 14
Präpositionen 66, 68, 70
Prepositions 66, 68, 70
Present Progressive 24, 25

Questions 36–39

Reading and Understanding 76

s-Genitive 10
Short Answers 37
Simple Past 26, 28
Simple Present 20, 22
Spickzettel 82
Statement 32
Subordinate Clauses 41

Time 50
to be 21

Uhrzeit 50

Verben mit zwei Objekten 34
Verbs with two Objects 34
Vergangenheit, einfache 26

Wh-Questions 38
Wörter singen 82
Wortfelder 83

Yes/No Questions 36

Zahlen 46
Zeitangaben 59

Bildnachweis

DigitalStock: S. 5 © P. Lange
PantherMedia: S. 31 © Stefan Willuda; S. 33 © Christian Fickinger
PIXELIO: S. 9 © Viviane Bourkel; S. 57 © Hans Altenkirch
PHOTOCASE: S. 19 © Patrik Naumann; S. 41 © lama-photography; S. 47 © boardbabe78; S. 71 © muffinmaker
Shutterstock: S. 12 © fckncg; S. 14 © steamroller_blues; S. 28 © kristian sekulic; S. 40 © Bruno Medley; S. 48 © goran cakmazovic; S. 51 (unten Mitte) © Happy Alex; S. 53 © Pertusinas; S. 60 © B.S. Karan; S. 61 © Peter Clark; S. 65 © WH Chow; S. 75 © Anna Chelnokova; S. 77 © Benson HE; S. 83 und 120 © Morgan Lane Photography; S. 85 und 121 © kristian sekulic; S. 88 © Andrjuss; S. 90 © Fedor Selivanov; S. 95 Jozsef Szasz-Fabian
www.fotolia.de: S. 14 © The Third Man; S. 21 © Piumadaquila; S. 23 © Antje Lindert-Rottke; S. 27 © Galina Barskaya; S. 45 © Phoenixpix; S. 51 (oben links) © Harris Shiffman; S. 51 (oben Mitte) © Mikko Pitkänen; S. 51 (unten links) © Udo Kroener; S. 51 (rechts) SwenG; S. 81 © Monkey Business; S. 86 © Aramanda; S. 87 © Esther Hildebrandt; S. 89 © Doreen Salcher; S. 117 © Iain Frazier

Illustrationen auf S. 7, 10, 50, 51, 58, 69, 91, 94, 96, 97 und 124 von **Ute Ohlms, Braunschweig**